BOUNCING BACK FROM BURNOUT

Bouncing Back from Burnout

KATHLEEN HARVEY

Bouncing Back from Burnout: The EA Handbook
© Kathleen Harvey 2025

All rights reserved. No part of this book may be copied, stored in a retrieval system, or transmitted in any form or by any means — electronic, mechanical, photocopying, recording, or otherwise — without the prior written permission of the publisher, except for brief quotations used in reviews and articles.

This book is a work of nonfiction. Every effort has been made to provide accurate and up-to-date information; however, the author and publisher make no guarantees about the effectiveness of any recommendations. The reader is responsible for their own decisions and outcomes. The author and publisher disclaim any liability for loss or damage resulting from the use of this book.

First published in Australia by Kathleen Harvey and David Whitbread
ISBN (Paperback): 978-1-7638812-1-1
ISBN (eBook): 978-1-7638812-2-8

Cover design by David Whitbread
Cover photo by nikamo/Shutterstock
Author portrait by John Harvey
Edited by David Whitbread

AI-Assisted tools were used in the research and editing of this book to enhance clarity and efficiency but all final content was curated by the author.

For more information, visit **www.theEAhandbook.com**

Legal Deposits & Copyright Notices (Australia & KDP Requirements)
A copy of this book will be deposited with the National Library of Australia in accordance with Australian legal deposit laws.

Amazon KDP editions are printed and distributed according to the terms and conditions of Kindle Direct Publishing

DISCLAIMER

The views, thoughts, and opinions expressed in *Bouncing Back from Burnout: The EA Handbook* are solely those of the author and do not necessarily reflect the views, policies, or positions of any past, present, or future employer, client, or affiliated organisation.

This book is based on personal experience and research, and it is intended for informational purposes only. It does not constitute professional, medical or legal advice. Readers should consult appropriate professionals for guidance tailored to their specific circumstances.

While every effort has been made to ensure the accuracy and completeness of the information contained in this book, the author and publisher assume no responsibility for errors, omissions or any outcomes resulting from the use of this material.

This book is for you.
It is a testament to the strength and skills you have forgotten are inside you.

CONTENTS

Preface		xi
Acknowledgements		xii
Introduction		1
	The unique position of the EA role	4

PART 1	**Identifying the problem**	7
CHAPTER 1	Bullying and burnout	9
CHAPTER 2	The EA–executive dynamic	17
CHAPTER 3	Locus of control	37

PART 2	**What to do if it happens to you**	47
CHAPTER 4	Finding the source	49
CHAPTER 5	Finding solutions	54
CHAPTER 6	Framing the conversation	63
CHAPTER 7	Documentation	67

PART 3	**Now what?**	73
CHAPTER 8	Deliberate healing	75
CHAPTER 9	The next right step	90

PART 4	**Tools**	99
CHAPTER 10	Embracing new technology	101
CHAPTER 11	Life audits	107
CHAPTER 12	Vision boards	128
CHAPTER 13	Boundaries worksheet	135
CHAPTER 14	Documenting conversations	140
CHAPTER 15	Brain dump template	143
Citations		148
About the author		151

PREFACE

Burnout is a word thrown around casually – but if you have picked up this book, you know it's more than feeling a bit tired. It's exhaustion that creeps into your bones.

It's cynicism that clouds your once-sharp business instincts, and a sense of being trapped in a role you once loved.

As Executive Assistants (EAs) we pride ourselves in keeping everything running smoothly.

What happens when we begin to break down?

I wrote *Bouncing Back from Burnout* because I've been there.

I know how it feels when the advice just doesn't fit the reality of our jobs. This book is here to help you recognise burnout and find ways to recover without walking away from the career you've built.

However, this book is not a substitute for professional support. If you're struggling, please reach out. Organisations like those below provide resources and support for mental health:

- **Beyond Blue** (1300 224 636)
- **Lifeline** (13 11 14)
- **Black Dog Institute** (www.blackdoginstitute.org.au)
- **Australian Psychological Society** (psychology.org.au)
  You are not alone, and help is available.

Burnout is not the end of your story. Let's start turning the page together.

ACKNOWLEDGEMENTS

This book wouldn't exist without the guidance, support and encouragement of so many people.

To my career coach Katrena Friel who encouraged me to write in the first place. Your belief in my voice gave me the courage to put words on a page.

To David Whitbread, whose keen eye and design experience shaped this book into something I am truly proud of. Your patience and dedication in this and all things made all the difference.

To my sister Maggie Whitbread-O'Brien who turned a professional eye to my work to ensure my research aligns with psychological methods. Your insights helped strengthen the book's foundation.

To the current and former Executives and EAs who shared their experiences with me. Your honesty, vulnerability and resilience inspire me daily.

And finally, to my husband John Harvey and our family and friends – your unwavering support and belief in me have been my anchor. Thank you for taking this journey with me.

I am so lucky to have such a spectacular community of people around me and I am so grateful to all of you.

INTRODUCTION

It came without warning. A storm I didn't see coming. One moment, I felt strong—I was speaking at conferences, mentoring new EAs. My resilience was something I had worked relentlessly to build over the years.

I thought I had done the work. I had fortified myself with boundaries, self-care practices and strategies to manage stress. I had created a life and routines where I felt stable, confident and capable.

But somehow, in what felt like the blink of an eye, everything unravelled. I was blindsided by how suddenly I was swept from that place of certainty and control, into an overwhelming sea of exhaustion and helplessness.

It wasn't just the workload or a particularly busy period of longer than usual hours, though both certainly played a role. It was the way the demands on me, from my executive and other people I worked closely with had slowly worn me down. The weight of responsibility became too much, and the cracks started to show. Before I knew it, I found myself spiralling in.

All of a sudden, my self-care strategies failed me, and I couldn't catch my breath before the burnout cycle took hold. The expectations continued to grow, the stress I felt at what I felt were my failures feeding into the cycle and compounding its impact on my sense of self and self-esteem.

Ultimately this burnout spiral made me vulnerable to bullying. The microaggressions and criticisms further eroded my confidence. The bullying and burnout fed off each other, leaving me in a place where I felt small, unappreciated, and ultimately broken. I felt I couldn't escape it.

The most shocking part for me was how easily it all happened. How quickly the strength I thought I had built could crumble. How the foundation I had worked so hard to establish could be shattered in what felt like an instant.

I had put so much time and effort into fortifying myself — only to watch it all unravel in the face of overwhelming demands, isolation and a lack of support.

It was a gut-wrenching realisation. But even more devastating was the absence of resources for someone in my position.

As an Executive Assistant (EA), there's no safety net. I can't reduce my workload; I can't just delegate tasks to others. I *am* the delegation point. There's noone else to pass the burden onto. Any attempt to push something back felt inadequate and, frankly, risky.

There was no clear path to relief — just the relentless march of responsibilities and stress.

I felt incredibly isolated in this experience. I felt trapped, caught between the need to uphold my responsibilities and the realisation that I was too far gone to manage on my own.

In a role that demands so much from you, the feeling of being alone in the struggle is overwhelming. There was no easy fix, no simple solution to my exhaustion, and no one who truly understood the unique pressures of being an EA. Not to mention the potential reputational damage to both me and my executive if I opened up about my experience.

It's a lonely place to be, and it's hard to know where to turn when the world around you expects you to always be 'on', even when you're barely holding it together.

I want to share the tools that helped me pull myself back to solid ground in the hopes that you don't feel so alone.

The purpose of this book is to give you the tools to fortify yourself against the unique and often invisible challenges of burnout.

As EAs, we are in a position that makes us particularly vulnerable to stress and exhaustion. The demands are high, the workload is relentless, and often our work goes unnoticed — until something goes wrong.

It's easy to feel like you're constantly being pulled in every direction, with no time or space to recharge. There's an insidious expectation that we should be able to handle it all, that we should somehow be impervious to the weight of the job.

But the truth is, sometimes it does get overwhelming—and that's OK. It's OK to feel like you've reached your limit. It's OK to admit that things are tough.

The goal here is to show you that even when you find yourself on the edge, there are ways to find your footing again. You don't need to completely uproot your life or change your entire professional situation to regain control.

Burnout can feel like a heavy, all-encompassing force, but there are actionable steps you can take to improve your situation, even if you can't yet imagine a full reset.

The idea of starting over—of walking away from your current executive relationship and beginning anew—can feel like a monumental task. In fact, when you're in the midst of burnout, the thought of starting over can feel more daunting than staying put. The thought of finding a new executive, building new rapport and navigating another relationship can feel like adding even more weight to an already burdensome load.

That's why, in this book, we focus on finding ways to improve your current circumstances. Sometimes the answer isn't to start from scratch, but to shift your current approach—making small, deliberate changes that help you regain balance and a sense of control.

It's about taking the time to acknowledge where you are, assess the situation with compassion, and then implement strategies that help you cope more effectively within your existing role.

By making these changes, you can build a healthier, more sustainable dynamic with your executive, protect your well-being and ultimately restore your energy without needing to completely overhaul your life.

This isn't about perfection; it's about progress—and learning that, even in the midst of chaos, there are ways to find peace.

The unique position of the EA role

The Executive Assistant (EA) role is unique in many ways. One of the most unusual aspects of the position is that it is inherently dependent on the success of another person.

Unlike other roles that function independently, the role of an EA cannot exist without an executive. It's a symbiotic relationship, where the work you do is intricately tied to the needs and demands of the executive you support.

At its core, the EA role is centred around this dynamic – the ebb and flow of communication, collaboration and mutual understanding. When the relationship between an EA and their executive is healthy, it creates a highly productive, efficient partnership.

The challenges arise, however, when that relationship begins to deteriorate, shift or become strained. A breakdown in communication or expectations can have a direct impact on the effectiveness of the EA role, making it harder to thrive in such an interdependent position.

The EA role is also notably social. Unlike many other positions, EAs often find themselves in almost a customer-facing role, dealing with internal and external stakeholders on a daily basis.

You are the first point of contact for many, coordinating meetings, managing schedules, and often acting as a liaison between your executive and the rest of the organisation. Because the role is so visible in terms of coordination and logistics, it requires exceptional people skills.

'A great executive doesn't "have" an EA, they partner with one. The difference is one burns out handling chaos they didn't create. The other thrives as a strategic ally shaping the future. If you want less burnout, start with better leadership.'
Jessica McBride
Founder of Tech Savvy Assistant & Co-Founder of The Future Focused Admin

The work you do, however, is often invisible to the untrained eye. When an EA does their job well, things run seamlessly, and that's often the end of the story — everything works, and no one realises how much effort went into making that happen.

This lack of recognition can be frustrating, especially when the role is performed at a high level with little acknowledgement. Ironically, it's often when something goes wrong that the spotlight is cast on the EA. Negative feedback, rather than positive reinforcement, can become more common, making it harder to gauge your performance in a meaningful way.

The lack of regular positive feedback is one of the major challenges of the EA role and can be a significant contributor to the development of burnout within the profession. Since so much of the work is done behind the scenes and often goes unnoticed, it can be difficult to know whether you're meeting expectations or excelling in your role. This lack of affirmation can create a sense of self-doubt or inadequacy, as the achievements of the role aren't always visible.

Over time, this can lead to feelings of impostor syndrome, where you may feel that you aren't truly qualified or deserving of your position, despite the fact that you're performing important tasks and keeping everything running smoothly.

Without regular, explicit feedback or appreciation, it's easy to internalise these feelings of doubt.

Moreover, the demanding nature of the EA role can lead to an overwhelming sense of isolation. Due to the separation of the executive from the teams and the professional boundary between the EA and the staff, EAs are often left without peers and without a support system within an organisation.

It is easy for EAs to become quite solitary. This is often compounded by a tendency for people to withdraw when they are experiencing burnout symptoms. The lack of close colleagues and a team can contribute to the burnout cycle by reducing your options for reprioritising and reducing the workload to allow space for recovery.

The role often comes with high visibility within the organisation, especially when things are running smoothly, but there is little support targeted specifically to the unique challenges that EAs face. The work can be incredibly demanding, both emotionally and mentally, as you balance multiple priorities, anticipate needs and manage a variety of tasks and people.

In such a high-stakes, high-pressure environment, it's important to recognise the need for support and resources that specifically cater to EAs, but unfortunately those resources are often limited and difficult to find.

The work may be emotionally taxing, and without proper tools or guidance, it can feel like you're navigating through it alone. Recognising this imbalance and seeking ways to address it is essential for maintaining both professional effectiveness and personal well-being.

PART 1
Identifying the problem

CHAPTER 1
Bullying and burnout

Burnout and bullying are two deeply intertwined issues that can fuel each other, creating a vicious cycle that's hard to break free from. It's easy to think of them as separate problems but, in reality, they often feed off one another, amplifying the damage they cause.

Burnout can lead to vulnerability—when you're mentally and physically drained, it becomes harder to maintain boundaries, assert your needs, or recognise when you're being mistreated.

This exhaustion and diminished resilience can leave you open to exploitation, and unfortunately some people may seize the opportunity to take advantage of your weakened state, using bullying tactics to further manipulate or control you.

Bullying contributes to burnout by adding to your emotional and mental stress. Constantly being undermined, belittled or pressured can take an enormous toll on your well-being, especially when it happens over an extended period. The relentlessness, unpredictability and anxiety bullying generate add to the overwhelm, making it more difficult to manage your workload, maintain positive relationships, and take care of your emotional needs.

What's worse is that the toxic environment created by bullying makes it harder for you to recover from burnout. It's a double hit that erodes both your professional and personal life, leaving you feeling drained, disempowered and increasingly isolated.

Because these two issues are so interconnected, it's crucial to address the root cause, rather than just treating the symptoms. If you're experiencing burnout but aren't able to recognise any external signs of bullying, it's important to ask yourself why you're feeling so overwhelmed.

Are there underlying power dynamics, unreasonable expectations, or personal attacks that you haven't yet fully acknowledged?

On the other hand, if you are dealing with bullying, it's essential to recognise how much this behaviour is contributing to your burnout. Sometimes, it's easy to blame yourself for feeling exhausted, like you're just not managing things well enough, but the reality is that the external pressures from bullying may be the very thing draining you.

Identifying which issue—burnout or bullying—is at the core of your struggle is crucial to taking effective action. Once you can pinpoint the underlying cause, you can begin to address it head-on, rather than simply trying to push through the exhaustion or trying to manage the symptoms.

Whether it's seeking support for bullying, setting stronger boundaries, or developing a plan to recover from burnout, understanding the source of your pain gives you the clarity you need to take control of the situation and find a path forward that restores your balance and well-being.

What is burnout?

Burnout is something that many of us may have heard of but perhaps don't fully understand until it hits. The World Health Organization (WHO) defines it as an 'occupational phenomenon' that arises from chronic workplace stress that hasn't been successfully managed.

It's not just about being tired or overworked; it's about a deep and persistent depletion of your energy, mental capacity and sense of self-worth at work. The symptoms of burnout are much more profound than simply feeling overwhelmed—though that is a part of it.

It manifests as an all-encompassing exhaustion, a constant mental fog and a growing sense of detachment or negativity toward your role. This detachment can even evolve into cynicism, where you begin to question not only the value of your work but also your place within it.

The impact of burnout isn't just emotional. It's physical, mental and even spiritual.

The exhaustion that comes with burnout is unlike regular fatigue. It's the kind of tiredness that doesn't fade after a weekend of rest or a good night's sleep. It seeps into your body and mind, leaving you feeling drained and incapable of summoning the energy to tackle even the simplest tasks.

You start to feel mentally distant from your work — like you're going through the motions, but there's no real connection anymore. This can breed feelings of frustration and, over time, make you less effective in your role and reduce your work performance overall.

The sharpness, the drive, the enthusiasm you once had all starts to erode, making it harder to perform at the high level you had come to expect from yourself.

In essence, burnout occurs when the demands of the job outweigh your mental, emotional and physical resources. It's a mismatch between what's required of you and what you're able to give.

The stress that builds up over time can become so overwhelming that you lose sight of why you're doing the work in the first place. As this disconnection deepens, so does the sense of self-doubt and the feeling that you're not making any meaningful impact. It's a vicious cycle that can spiral quickly, especially in roles like that of an Executive Assistant where the weight of others' expectations can press on you heavily.

Burnout doesn't happen overnight, but it can hit with shocking force when it reaches its peak. Understanding what burnout looks like and how it affects you is the first step in taking control and seeking solutions before it becomes all-consuming.

How do I know if it's happening to me?

Recognising the signs of burnout can be difficult because it often creeps up on you slowly, like a shadow that gets longer and longer until it completely overtakes the light.

At first, it may feel like something is just 'off', but you can't pinpoint exactly what's wrong. One of the earliest signs that burnout is happening is the gradual erosion of your self-esteem and self-worth.

It's subtle at first, you miss a couple of deadlines, feel a little scatterbrained or find it difficult to focus, or just feel like you're not doing your best work. But soon, those moments pile up, and you start to feel like you're just not measuring up anymore. This nagging feeling that you're somehow falling short can chip away at your confidence and cause you to question your value both at work and as a person.

Another common sign of burnout is withdrawal. You may find yourself retreating from activities and people that once brought you joy or fulfillment. What once felt like a lively and rewarding social life now feels draining, and even though you know you should stay connected, you choose to isolate yourself.

You may avoid reaching out to colleagues or friends, opting to stay in your own space and not engage. This 'hibernation' is often a coping mechanism, a way to protect yourself from the emotional overload. However, in the long run, this withdrawal can deepen feelings of isolation and contribute to the negative spiral that burnout creates.

Burnout may also manifest in changes to your executive functioning—the mental processes that allow you to plan, make decisions, focus and complete tasks efficiently.

You may notice that it's harder to concentrate, your decision-making feels sluggish, or you become overwhelmed by tasks that once felt easy to manage. Even simple tasks can become mountains to climb, and your ability to prioritise may deteriorate.

It's as if your brain is constantly in overdrive, unable to rest or recalibrate. Your focus and productivity decline, and the pressure of not being able to perform at your usual level only adds to the frustration.

Some of the early warning signs to look for if you think you might be experiencing burnout are:

- **Chronic fatigue**: feeling drained or exhausted even after a full night's sleep
- **Decreased productivity**: struggling to handle tasks or activities at work that you have previously managed easily

- **Emotional exhaustion**: feeling overwhelmed and stressed more often; sometimes this looks like unusually sudden and extreme mood swings
- **Difficulty focusing**: trouble staying on task or concentrating even on routine or simple tasks
- **Physical symptoms**: more frequent headaches, muscle pain or tension, digestive problems and other unexplained physical issues
- **Feelings of disconnection**: a sense of disconnection from work, relationships and sense of self, in some cases this can become a sense of unreality or dissociation[1]
- **Increased negativity**: you may notice you are feeling more negative towards your job, your colleagues or the business you work for
- **Sleep disturbances**: increased difficulty falling asleep or staying asleep, an inability to 'switch off'
- **Discontent**: feeling less fulfilled or happy about different aspects of your life, even when you are celebrating achievements and accomplishments
- **Avoiding work**: you may be more prone to procrastination or avoiding your responsibilities.

If you are noticing a few of these symptoms beginning to impact, it might be time to begin taking preventative steps. Being proactive and addressing the source of your burnout early is critical to preserving your well-being and continuing to be productive in your role.

After all the hard work you've put in to build yourself up — to be strong, capable and confident — it can feel devastating to suddenly find yourself struggling. You might be blindsided by how quickly things unravelled, wondering why it feels so overwhelming when you thought you were resilient.

---

[1] Dissociation is an involuntary feeling of disconnectedness, as distinct from disassociation which is conscious or voluntary disconnection from an event or reality. Both are relevant but should be considered distinct.

The emotional toll can leave you feeling like a shell of who you once were, questioning your ability to cope and even your worthiness for the role you've always embraced.

This sense of vulnerability can be difficult to accept, but it's important to acknowledge it as part of the process of healing. Only by recognising that burnout has taken hold can you begin to take proactive steps toward recovery.

What is bullying?

Bullying in the workplace is not just about one-off moments of conflict or disagreement; it's the repeated, intentional targeting of an individual through harmful or aggressive actions.

At its core, bullying is about power—specifically, an imbalance of power. The bully seeks to assert control over their target, using tactics like force, coercion, hurtful teasing or threats.

It's not a momentary lapse in judgement or a misunderstanding, but rather a calculated, persistent attempt to dominate or intimidate.

Bullying can occur on a spectrum, from overt aggression to more subtle, insidious forms of emotional manipulation. But what all forms have in common is that they erode the target's sense of security, confidence, and sense of self.

One of the key elements that distinguishes bullying from ordinary workplace conflict is this imbalance of power. In any relationship, disagreements are bound to happen, but they can often be resolved through communication, compromise, or simple confrontation.

Bullying, on the other hand, is characterised by the consistent use of power to hurt, dominate or control. It may be physical, such as in situations where an executive or colleague uses their physical presence or strength to intimidate, or it may be emotional, where subtle manipulation and constant undermining erode the victim's confidence and sense of autonomy.

The key difference here is that, in bullying, the victim is often made to feel helpless and incapable of changing their circumstances, adding to the long-lasting psychological damage that this behaviour can cause.

For Executive Assistants, bullying can often take a more nuanced form. Because the role often involves being in a position of support, the target of bullying may not always be immediately obvious to others in the organisation. It could be subtle demands, constant micromanagement, or negative remarks that, while not overtly abusive, create a toxic environment. The perception of powerlessness is what makes this behaviour particularly harmful.

When you feel that your ability to advocate for yourself is stifled by the very dynamics of your role, it can be challenging to recognise and respond to bullying. However, it is essential to acknowledge that this type of behaviour is not only damaging to your professional growth but to your mental and emotional well-being as well.

Understanding what bullying looks like and how it manifests is the first step in protecting yourself. Bullying is never about your worth or ability — it is about the toxic imbalance of power that makes it difficult for the victim to stand up for themselves.

Recognising these signs early, whether it's subtle remarks, unmanageable expectations, or consistent undermining, can help you take action before the situation becomes more entrenched.

Noone should have to endure bullying at work, and by learning to identify it, you give yourself the chance to address the issue, seek support and create the healthy, balanced work environment you deserve.

Not all behaviour that makes a person feel upset or undervalued at work is workplace bullying. Examples of behaviours, whether intentional or unintentional, that may be considered workplace bullying if they are repeated, unreasonable and create a risk to health and safety include, but are not limited to:

- abusive, insulting or offensive language or comments
- aggressive and intimidating conduct
- belittling or humiliating comments

- practical jokes or initiation (including hazing)
- unjustified criticism or complaints
- deliberately excluding someone from work-related activities
- withholding information that is vital for effective work performance
- setting unreasonable timelines or constantly changing deadlines (with no clear business reason)
- deliberately setting tasks that are unreasonably beyond a person's skill level without providing appropriate support and resources for the person to reasonably be expected to complete the task
- denying or obscuring access to information or resources to the detriment of the worker
- spreading misinformation or malicious rumours
- changing work arrangements, such as rosters and leave, to deliberately inconvenience a particular worker or workers.

If the behaviour involves violence, for example physical assault or the threat of physical assault, it should be reported to the police.[2]

---

[2] This passage on behaviours that may be considered workplace bullying has been adapted from SafeWork Australia (2016), *Dealing With Workplace Bullying: A Worker's Guide*

CHAPTER 2
The EA–executive dynamic

Executive Assistants play a unique and vital role in the workplace, often acting as the silent force that keeps the wheels turning behind the scenes. We balance multiple competing priorities, manage time-sensitive demands and help our executives stay organised in the face of ever-shifting schedules and objectives.

This job requires a remarkable set of skills, including exceptional emotional intelligence (EQ), discretion, adaptability and a deep sense of professionalism. However, while these qualities are indispensable in fostering a productive workplace, they can also make EAs more susceptible to burnout when not carefully managed.

Many EAs naturally possess a high level of emotional intelligence, allowing us to understand and respond to the emotions and needs of others with sensitivity and diplomacy. Often introverted and reserved, we excel in maintaining harmony and navigating complex interpersonal dynamics. These traits enable us to manage relationships effectively and provide crucial support to our executives.

However, these same qualities, when taken to an extreme, can also create challenges for EAs, particularly when we struggle to advocate for our own well-being. The desire to maintain a positive atmosphere and avoid conflict often leads to people-pleasing behaviours — such as saying 'yes' to every request, even when it's not feasible or healthy. Over time, this can contribute to overwork, overwhelm and eventually burnout.

The high standards EAs set for ourselves only add to the potential for exhaustion. Many EAs take great pride in our ability to anticipate our executive's needs, striving for excellence and efficiency in all we do. We often go above and beyond to ensure that everything runs smoothly, seamlessly anticipating issues before they arise, and managing complex tasks without missing a beat.

While this dedication is admirable, it can lead to neglecting our own physical and emotional needs. Long hours, skipped meals, and the constant pressure of an ever-growing to-do list can begin to take a toll.

Moreover, because EAs often work behind the scenes, our contributions may go unrecognised — not due to a lack of appreciation, but because our efficiency and ability to make difficult tasks look effortless can inadvertently make our role invisible.

On the other side of this partnership, executives typically exhibit a different set of traits that have helped them rise to leadership positions.

They are often assertive, outcome-focused, and highly driven, qualities that are critical for decision-making and achieving business objectives. These traits can be incredibly effective in pushing teams to perform at a high level and driving organisational success.

However, this strong focus on results and achievement can sometimes come at the expense of the human element — such as the well-being of their teams and the emotional impact their decisions might have.

'A strong EA/executive partnership isn't a "nice to have" – it's essential. When there's mutual respect, clear boundaries, and space to be human, EAs thrive. But when that balance is off, burnout isn't far behind. We're strategic operators. And that kind of responsibility deserves a workplace that has our backs.'
Candice Burningham
Founder of Admin Avenues & Co-Founder of The Future Focused Admin

For EAs, this dynamic can be particularly challenging. Executives may not always realise the full scope of the administrative burden they place on their assistant. Their dominant, assertive personalities, while essential for leadership, can sometimes make it harder for us as EAs to set boundaries or push back when the workload becomes overwhelming.

The executive might not recognise how much they are demanding of their EA, especially if the EA is constantly striving to meet expectations and avoid conflict.

Additionally, the nature of the EA role often involves a high degree of emotional labour. EAs are not only managing schedules and logistics — they are also managing relationships, emotions and expectations.

We often serve as a buffer between our executives and the rest of the organisation, absorbing stress, defusing conflicts and maintaining a sense of calm in the midst of chaos. While this 'invisible' work is critical to the smooth functioning of the workplace, it can also be deeply draining and contributes significantly to burnout if not managed properly.

Despite these challenges, when the EA–executive partnership is well-balanced, it becomes a powerful and productive unit. The EA's emotional intelligence, attention to detail and ability to manage relationships can complement the executive's assertiveness, vision and focus on results.

Together, they can ensure that both the strategic and human elements of leadership are addressed, creating a dynamic where productivity is enhanced without sacrificing well-being. This type of collaboration allows the executive to stay focused on high-level objectives while the EA keeps everything aligned and organised.

'The Executive and EA must work together as a team, foreseeing the needs and challenges of the other – having ESP is not mandatory but would help. The challenge of the EA is to remove the mundane from the Exec's day to allow them to focus on delivering the outcomes for which they are employed.'
Stuart McKinnon
Retired Assistant Secretary, Australian Public Service, 21 March 2025

Creating and maintaining this kind of partnership takes ongoing effort and commitment from both parties. It requires open communication, mutual respect and a shared understanding of each other's strengths and blind spots.

EAs must feel empowered to set boundaries, ask for help, and push back when necessary, without fearing that it will harm the professional relationship.

Executives in turn must be mindful of their EA's workload and the pressures they face, recognising that their well-being is just as critical to the team's success as the work they produce.

There are several practical steps that can help foster a balanced and supportive working relationship. Regular check-ins to discuss workload, priorities and potential roadblocks can prevent misunderstandings and ensure that your capacity is not overextended.

Clear expectations around response times, availability and what constitutes an urgent matter can help establish boundaries and reduce the risk of burnout. You should also feel comfortable flagging when you're approaching your capacity for additional work or need support, so adjustments can be made proactively.

For EAs who may already be experiencing burnout, it's essential to prioritise self-care and advocate for a more balanced approach to their role. This might involve having open, honest conversations with your executive about workload, delegating tasks, and seeking support from colleagues or mentors.

Finding strategies to manage stress effectively—whether through mindfulness, exercise or creative outlets—can also play a crucial role in preventing burnout. Taking time to step away and recharge, whether through short breaks during the day or using vacation time, is not a luxury but a necessity for long-term productivity and mental health.

By fostering a collaborative and supportive working relationship, EAs and executives can create a partnership that thrives on balance and mutual respect. With intentional effort and open communication, both parties can ensure that their working relationship remains productive, respectful and sustainable, fostering a healthier work environment where both individuals feel valued and empowered.

The hidden cost of burnout on your EA-executive partnership

As Executive Assistants, we pride ourselves on being the steady, reliable force behind our executives – anticipating needs, managing priorities and keeping the office running smoothly. But when burnout creeps in it can erode the foundation of our partnership with our executives.

Burnout often manifests as exhaustion, disengagement and a sense of overwhelm. When it happens, it can become harder to maintain the high level of support our roles demand. Communication is often the first casualty of EA burnout.

Our attention to detail slips, our ability to anticipate needs and think strategically wanes. We lose the ability to advocate for ourselves and set healthy boundaries. This can lead to misunderstandings and growing frustration on both sides. The trust we worked so hard to build, a cornerstone of our partnerships, begins to feel the strain.

We take on more than we can possibly manage fearing that pushing back and saying no will let our executive down. In reality, operating from a place of burnout diminishes the quality of our work, and our ability to provide thoughtful, proactive support to our usual standard.

Acknowledging burnout and its impact on your capacity isn't a weakness. It's a step towards preserving the partnership and allows us to deliver for our teams. By prioritising our own wellbeing, we strengthen our ability to show up fully, collaborate effectively and maintain the trust and respect essential to a thriving EA-Executive partnership.

When we are honest about our workload, capacity and even our moments of vulnerability, we create space for more open and constructive communication and allow the executive to feel comfortable communicating the same issues with us.

This honesty fosters mutual respect and helps us to better understand our executives and how we can best support each other. It sets the stage for more realistic expectations and collaborative problem-solving, ensuring both sides feel heard and valued. In the long run, this openness not only strengthens trust but also builds a healthier, more resilient working relationship.

How DiSC personality traits shape EA–executive partnerships

The DiSC personality assessment is a widely recognised and trusted tool that helps individuals understand their behavioural styles and how they interact with others in the workplace.

The assessment divides personalities into four primary traits — Dominance (D), Influence (i), Steadiness (S), and Conscientiousness (C). Each of these traits influences how a person communicates, makes decisions and approaches challenges, providing a unique lens through which to understand both themselves and others. By analysing these core traits, DiSC allows individuals to gain deeper insights into their own work styles as well as those of the people they interact with.

For EAs and their executives, understanding the DiSC model can be incredibly beneficial. As an EA, your role requires flexibility, adaptability, and a deep understanding of both the needs of the executive and the wider team. When you understand the specific personality traits of both yourself and your executive, it allows for more effective communication, clearer expectations and smoother collaboration.

It's about knowing how to adapt your approach to best suit your executive's personality and work style, while also recognising how your own traits might influence how you work together. This mutual understanding can help reduce misunderstandings, avoid friction and foster a healthier, more harmonious working relationship.

Recognising and embracing the differences in personality styles doesn't just improve communication; it also leads to greater respect and empathy within the working dynamic. When both the EA and the executive understand and appreciate each other's strengths and challenges, they can work together to create a more efficient and supportive partnership.

For example, an executive who scores high in Dominance may appreciate an EA who is assertive and can make decisions quickly, while an EA with a Steadiness trait may bring a calm, patient and people-focused approach to the table. Similarly, an EA with strong Conscientiousness (C) traits can offer precision and attention to detail, balancing out an executive who might be more driven by big-picture goals. Together, they can create a balanced, effective and supportive work environment that benefits not just their professional relationship, but the entire organisation.

Understanding DiSC ultimately enables both the EA and the executive to maximise their strengths, complement each other's weaknesses, and achieve their shared goals in a more mindful and productive way.

The strength of steadiness

EAs often naturally display strong Steadiness (S) traits. These individuals are known for their patience, reliability and empathetic approach to work. They thrive in collaborative environments and excel at maintaining harmony and stability, especially in high-pressure situations.

Their ability to remain calm and supportive under stress makes them invaluable in their roles, often acting as the glue that holds teams together. Furthermore, their high emotional intelligence enables them to navigate workplace dynamics with tact, sensitivity and diplomacy, all of which are essential qualities for supporting executives effectively.

However, the very strengths that make S-type EAs so exceptional can also create challenges and vulnerabilities. Their deep desire to maintain peace and avoid conflict may prevent them from addressing issues in real time, even when they're faced with unreasonable demands or mistreatment. Over time, this tendency to avoid confrontation can lead to burnout, as the weight of unresolved issues builds up.

Moreover, EAs with strong S traits may find it difficult to advocate for themselves, often prioritising others' needs over their own, which can exacerbate feelings of overwhelm and fatigue. For example, an EA with strong S traits may be hesitant to ask for help when overwhelmed, or they may tolerate working extra hours, even when it negatively impacts their health, in an effort to maintain peace.

Stepping into assertiveness

For many EAs, stepping into the assertiveness and directness associated with the Dominance (D) trait doesn't come as naturally. However, learning to embrace these elements can be transformative.

Assertiveness is crucial for managing your workload, setting boundaries, and maintaining a healthy, sustainable professional relationship with your executive. By incorporating D-trait skills, you will feel more comfortable pushing back when needed, have challenging conversations, and advocate for your own well-being without feeling like you're causing friction.

Developing assertiveness requires intentional practice. You can begin by identifying specific situations where you feel overburdened or undervalued, and then work on developing clear, respectful language to communicate your needs. For example, when an executive requests urgent tasks during a busy period, an EA with well-developed D-traits might directly explain how they will prioritise their responsibilities including tasks that may need to be abandoned or delayed to meet deadlines effectively.

Role-playing difficult conversations with a trusted mentor or colleague, setting small achievable goals for asserting boundaries, and even practicing positive self-talk can help bolster your confidence in navigating these situations.

Strengthening D-trait skills may not happen overnight, but with persistence, it can help you feel more empowered and in control of your professional life.

Balancing drive and respect

When the balance between assertiveness and empathy is not properly managed by your executive, you may begin to feel that your needs are being overlooked. It's important for you to understand that this is not always intentional, but it's the nature of many leadership roles to be focused on achieving goals and driving progress.

An executive with high Dominance traits, may be quick to make decisions and move onto the next task, sometimes unintentionally overlooking the feelings of their team. Nevertheless, it's crucial for you to develop strategies for asserting your own boundaries and needs in these situations. Being able to communicate effectively with an executive who may not fully appreciate the emotional toll of their demands is essential.

You also need to recognise that your relationship with your executive is symbiotic—both parties rely on one another. To maintain a healthy dynamic, EAs must take the time to express their needs, whether it's about workload management, clarity on priorities, or a respectful work environment, and executives must be able to do the same without damaging the partnership.

It's important to approach these conversations from a place of self-awareness, using clear, assertive language to set boundaries while maintaining the respect and professionalism that is expected in your respective roles.

Recognising the impact of your executive's Dominance (D) traits will also help you understand the need to engage in these conversations with empathy and a solutions-oriented approach.

The key is finding balance: ensuring that both the executive's need for results and the EA's need for respect and well-being are addressed in a way that supports the long-term success of both parties.

Using the DiSC personality types to strengthen the EA–executive partnership

Strengthening the EA–executive partnership begins with an understanding of the unique personality traits each person brings to the table and how you can balance each other to create a more rounded and balanced unit.

For your executive, their natural drive and tendency toward Dominance (D) traits can bring efficiency, clarity and decisive leadership to the workplace. These qualities are invaluable for pushing the organisation forward and meeting high-level goals, but they may sometimes come at the cost of focusing too heavily on results and forgetting the human aspect of the relationship with their staff.

An executive with strong D traits might not always be aware of how their direct approach can feel intimidating, or how a fast-paced, goal-oriented attitude can inadvertently push their teams toward overwhelm.

This is where your S traits become critical in creating balance. You can help your executive understand the importance of empathy and recognition of the emotional and physical toll that the work demands, which will contribute to the overall success of the partnership.

Open communication plays a pivotal role in bridging the gap between these personality differences. As an EA, it's important to clearly communicate how your executive's approach impacts your well-being, while also creating an environment where you feel empowered to ask for the resources or support you need.

Often your C and i personality traits also play a role in how you communicate most effectively. For example, during a busy week, an EA with high Conscientiousness might need more time to prepare detailed reports, while an executive with high Influence might require updates more frequently and in a less formal format.

Check-ins are essential to ensure that both parties are on the same page and that the workload and expectations are aligned. Your ability to express your needs—and the executive's willingness to listen—sets the stage for a healthy, effective and mutually supportive partnership. Through regular conversations about workload, boundaries and working styles, you can create an ongoing dialogue that enables both of you to thrive.

When you and your executive leverage the insights from the DiSC assessment, the benefits are far-reaching. The key is not to change each other's core traits but to understand and adapt to one another's styles. You can use this understanding to find common ground, strengthening both your relationship and your working dynamics.

In practice, this means that as an EA, you learn to set healthy boundaries while recognising that your executive's results-driven attitude comes from a place of ambition and leadership. Meanwhile, your executive can use their understanding of your more empathetic, people-focused traits to communicate in ways that encourage collaboration without pushing you too far.

This mutual respect for each other's strengths and challenges creates an environment where you can both flourish. By incorporating DiSC insights into your daily workflow, you ensure that the relationship stays balanced, supporting both professional goals and personal well-being. The result is a productive partnership where both parties feel respected, valued and empowered to do their best work.

Understanding and respecting the nuances of each other's personality traits allows you to create a working dynamic that is sustainable, fulfilling and ultimately drives success while prioritising well-being.

Interdependence vs codependence in the EA–executive partnership

Interdependence represents a balanced and healthy dynamic in which both parties rely on and support each other while maintaining their own autonomy and sense of self.

In an EA and executive partnership, interdependence means that each individual brings their unique strengths, skills and perspectives to the table. The relationship thrives on collaboration, where both the

EA and executive understand and respect each other's boundaries, needs and responsibilities. Each party contributes to the overall success of the partnership, and both parties are empowered to work toward shared goals while preserving their individuality.

For an EA, this type of relationship allows you to effectively manage your responsibilities, communicate openly about your needs, and assert your boundaries — without feeling guilty or overextended. You can offer support to the executive while also being mindful of your own well-being and personal space.

When both parties are aligned in their commitment to mutual respect and understanding, interdependence fosters a strong, productive working relationship that doesn't require sacrificing one person's needs for the other's.

On the other hand, codependence occurs when the needs, feelings and responsibilities of one person become overly entangled with the other's in an unhealthy manner.

In a codependent EA–executive partnership, the EA may continually prioritise the executive's demands, often at the expense of their own well-being. This might manifest in taking on an excessive workload, saying 'yes' to every request without considering personal limits, or feeling responsible for managing the executive's emotions and stress. The EA might feel compelled to meet every demand, even when it undermines their own health, time or productivity.

Over time, this codependent dynamic can lead to feelings of resentment, burnout and diminished effectiveness. The EA may start to feel that their own needs are secondary, leading to physical and emotional exhaustion. Meanwhile, the executive may inadvertently come to rely too heavily on the EA, which can create an unhealthy imbalance in the relationship. The underlying issue in a codependent partnership is the lack of boundaries, leading to an overwhelming sense of responsibility for the other person's well-being and outcomes.

The key difference between interdependence and codependence lies in the balance of power, responsibility and respect.

In an interdependent relationship, both the EA and the executive work together as equal partners who each maintain their own autonomy while collaborating effectively. There is a mutual understanding that both parties are responsible for their own well-being and productivity, and there is respect for personal boundaries.

In contrast, a codependent relationship breeds imbalance, with one person becoming over-reliant on the other, which can lead to exhaustion and resentment.

Ultimately, fostering an interdependent relationship allows both the EA and the executive to thrive individually and as a team. It's about creating a healthy, sustainable partnership that encourages mutual respect, shared responsibility and clear boundaries, enabling both parties to contribute to the organisation's success without compromising their personal well-being.

Building an interdependent EA–executive partnership: the key to long-term success

Some of the most effective and sustainable dynamics in the workplace are interdependent partnerships, where both parties bring their strengths to the table while also maintaining their individual autonomy. For you and your executive, cultivating this kind of relationship is vital to not only achieving organisational goals but also preserving both personal productivity and well-being.

An interdependent partnership creates a foundation of mutual respect, where collaboration thrives, yet each person's unique roles and boundaries are honoured. It fosters an environment where both you and the executive feel empowered, supported and valued.

But what does an interdependent partnership actually look like? And how can EAs and their executives establish one that encourages long-term success without slipping into unhealthy patterns?

At its core, an interdependent relationship is one where both parties are committed to understanding and supporting each other, while also recognising that both individuals have their own responsibilities, needs and limits.

This means that while the EA provides valuable support to the executive, they also have the right to manage their own time, energy and well-being. Likewise, the executive needs to acknowledge and respect the EA's boundaries, communicate openly about expectations, and trust the EA's expertise in managing the workload.

To establish such a partnership, clear communication is key. EAs and executives must have honest conversations about what each person's role entails, what the expectations are, and where boundaries need to be set.

This includes discussing priorities, deadlines and personal boundaries, as well as being proactive about anticipating challenges and addressing them together. For example, an EA might express the need for protected off-hours or time for personal commitments, while an executive might clarify what they consider urgent or important.

By having these candid discussions, both parties can avoid misunderstandings and foster a working relationship based on trust and mutual respect.

An interdependent partnership also requires flexibility and adaptability. The needs and demands of the workplace can evolve, and both you and the executive must be willing to adjust as necessary to maintain balance. This might mean renegotiating priorities or workload distribution in response to changing circumstances or new projects.

In such an environment, you will feel less like you are being dictated to, and more like you are involved in the management of the workload. The executive is supported by a proactive and reliable partner rather than barking orders.

The challenge in creating and maintaining an interdependent relationship is ensuring that both parties stay vigilant against slipping into unhealthy patterns.

If the balance tips too far in one direction, such as the EA consistently overextending themselves at the expense of their own well-being or the executive becoming overly reliant on the EA, it can lead to burnout, resentment and diminished productivity for either party. Therefore, an ongoing commitment to mutual respect, open communication and boundary-setting is essential. Both the EA and the executive must regularly check in with each other to make sure the partnership remains balanced and that neither party's needs or well-being are being compromised.

In essence, an interdependent partnership is about creating a dynamic that allows both the EA and the executive to thrive together — each contributing their expertise, respecting each other's space, and continually adjusting to ensure that the relationship remains supportive and sustainable. When this balance is struck, both productivity and well-being are elevated, leading to greater success for the individuals and the organisation.

Strengthening the partnership

An interdependent EA–executive relationship takes ongoing effort and communication. Regular check-ins, transparent conversations about workload and expectations, and mutual respect for each other's time and expertise lay the foundation for a balanced and sustainable partnership.

By embracing interdependence, both EAs and executives benefit from a relationship built on trust, respect and shared success — one that supports productivity without sacrificing well-being.

To build a stronger partnership, it's essential to develop a deeper understanding of your executive's professional and personal goals.

Take the time to learn about their long-term vision and immediate objectives, as this will allow you to anticipate needs and proactively support them in achieving these goals. For example, if you understand that your executive values time for strategic thinking, you can help block out distractions and protect that time by managing their calendar efficiently.

Become a strategic thought partner. When you're aware of the bigger picture of their goals and the company's mission, you can offer insights or suggest alternatives that align with those priorities. This could involve identifying opportunities to improve processes, saving time by recommending tools or strategies, or simply offering solutions to challenges before they become significant issues.

Your ability to think ahead will make you an invaluable resource, not just an assistant.

Building rapport is another crucial aspect of strengthening your partnership. This goes beyond just working well together on a professional level—understanding your executive's work habits, personality, and even their stress triggers can help you tailor your approach. For example, if they're someone who thrives with detailed information, you can ensure they receive reports with thorough data. If they appreciate brevity, providing succinct summaries might be more effective.

Another element to consider is emotional intelligence. Being able to read between the lines when things are getting stressful or challenging can make a huge difference.

If your executive is overwhelmed, offering a calming presence or suggesting ways to redistribute tasks or delegate effectively can help ease their stress and prevent burnout.

Additionally, empathy plays a big role in maintaining a productive and positive working relationship. Acknowledge their achievements, and don't hesitate to offer praise when they do something noteworthy. This helps create a supportive environment where both parties feel valued.

Lastly, working on improving your own personal development and skills will also make a difference. The more you invest in improving your technical abilities or learning new tools, the more value you can offer to your executive.

Whether it's enhancing your knowledge of project management software, honing your communication skills, or learning about industry trends, staying on top of your own growth will make you a stronger ally in their corner.

In essence, strengthening the partnership with your executive is about becoming more than just someone who organises their calendar or responds to emails. It's about understanding the bigger picture, offering support and insights that align with their goals, and fostering a relationship built on trust, respect and mutual understanding.

Setting clear and healthy boundaries

Setting clear and healthy boundaries in an EA–executive partnership is essential for fostering a sustainable and effective working relationship. As an EA, you are often at the centre of managing tasks, schedules and communications, which can quickly lead to feeling overextended if your boundaries aren't respected.

Without clear boundaries, there's a tendency for the lines between personal time and work time to blur, leading to burnout, frustration and decreased productivity.

Setting boundaries isn't about rejecting work or disengaging from responsibilities; it's about protecting your energy, time and well-being, so that you can be at your best for both yourself and your executive.

Healthy boundaries also allow you to manage expectations in a way that prevents resentment from building up over time. By having open conversations with your executive about what is and isn't acceptable in terms of workload, work hours and personal space, you're establishing a mutual understanding that enhances the working dynamic.

When both you and your executive are clear about what's expected, it becomes easier to prioritise tasks, avoid unnecessary stress and maintain a balanced relationship that respects both personal and professional needs. This clarity ensures that neither of you feels overwhelmed or unsupported, and it helps the partnership remain productive and positive.

For you as the EA, setting boundaries is also an act of self-advocacy. It requires recognising your own needs and communicating them in a way that is respectful but firm.

This process can be uncomfortable, especially in the face of a strong, results-driven executive. However, by asserting your boundaries, you are ensuring that you aren't overburdened, that your work is manageable, and that your physical and emotional well-being are safeguarded.

Without boundaries, the EA role can become all-consuming, leading to diminished job satisfaction, damage to your home life and personal relationships, and ultimately to burnout. When you set limits, you preserve your ability to perform at a high level and to continue contributing meaningfully to the success of the team and the organisation.

Boundaries also cultivate a more balanced power dynamic in the partnership. When both you and your executive understand and respect each other's limits, it creates a sense of fairness and mutual respect.

It's not about creating distance or being inflexible, but rather about ensuring that both parties have the space and clarity to do their best work without sacrificing personal health or happiness. With clear boundaries in place, you can navigate challenges with more confidence and have the emotional resilience needed to manage the demands of the role. This balance ultimately leads to a stronger, more effective partnership, where both you and your executive can thrive.

Where should I start setting boundaries?

While it may not be possible to negotiate in all partnerships, one of the most impactful and empowering boundaries for Executive Assistants is the right to disconnect.

In today's fast-paced work environment, where priorities shift rapidly and high-stakes demands are the norm, it can be incredibly difficult to maintain a clear distinction between work and personal life. The constant influx of requests, emails and messages can often lead to the blurring of these boundaries, leaving EAs feeling like they're always 'on' and never able to truly unplug.

This lack of separation can contribute to burnout and diminished well-being, making it even more important to assert and protect your right to disconnect.

Establishing clear and healthy boundaries around after-hours availability and response times is key to maintaining a balanced life. For instance, you might decide to set a clear expectation that you will only respond to after-hours communications in truly urgent situations.

The next step is to ensure your executive fully understands what constitutes an 'urgent' matter. This may mean you negotiate an agreed definition of what would be an emergency or time-sensitive issue. This could include things like critical meetings, last-minute travel arrangements, or issues that directly affect the day's operations.

By proactively communicating these expectations—and doing so consistently—you can preserve your work–life balance without feeling the pressure to be constantly available.

Open dialogue about what 'urgent' means—and what can wait—ensures that both you and your executive are aligned, preventing potential misunderstandings or unnecessary stress. Setting this boundary not only protects your time but also promotes a culture of respect for personal space, contributing to a healthier, more sustainable working relationship.

Having the right to disconnect doesn't just serve as a practical tool for avoiding and recovering from burnout; it also sends a message that personal time is valuable and must be protected.

With clear guidelines in place, you can more effectively navigate the demands of your role while still carving out space for yourself and your loved ones. Ultimately, this balance helps to foster both professional productivity and personal well-being, creating a more fulfilling and sustainable career path.

It's crucial to understand that boundaries are not tools to control others, but rather frameworks to help you manage your own well-being and reactions in different situations. Boundaries act as a guide for how you will respond if those limits are not respected, allowing you to maintain a sense of structure and balance, even in challenging scenarios.

For EAs, this concept is especially important as they often juggle multiple demands from their executives and colleagues. It can be easy to feel overwhelmed when expectations shift or when someone repeatedly disregards your personal boundaries.

For example, let's say an executive continues to send non-urgent emails or requests outside the agreed-upon working hours. Rather than allowing frustration to build up or reacting impulsively, the EA can approach this situation with a clear plan. The EA might decide to address these non-urgent requests the next business day, setting the expectation that work communications should occur during designated hours.

Alternatively, if the pattern persists, the EA can initiate a calm and constructive conversation with their executive to realign on boundaries and expectations, emphasising the importance of mutual respect for each other's time.

One of the most effective ways to manage your boundaries is by communicating proactively. This means setting clear expectations with your executive and colleagues early on, before a situation has the chance to escalate.

For example, if you're feeling overwhelmed with your workload, expressing your capacity in a respectful, solution-oriented manner can help prevent misunderstandings or unrealistic expectations from being placed on you.

Clear communication helps prevent the stress of unspoken expectations from building up and allows you to address potential issues before they become problems. This approach not only helps you preserve your boundaries but also creates space for open and respectful dialogue where both parties feel heard, validated and respected.

There are some worksheets at the end of this book to help you get started with setting boundaries in your workplace.

CHAPTER 3
Locus of control

The key to maintaining healthy boundaries lies in focusing on your locus of control—the aspects of the situation that you can directly influence or manage.

In the high-pressure, constantly shifting world of an EA, there is often a temptation to try to control or fix other people's actions or reactions. However, this focus can lead to frustration, burnout and unnecessary conflict.

Instead, when you shift your energy toward managing your own responses and actions, you regain a sense of agency and control over your work environment. By doing so, you empower yourself to maintain your boundaries in a way that fosters respect, collaboration and professional growth.

What is the locus of control?

Locus of control is a psychological concept that refers to the extent to which individuals believe they have control over the events that impact their lives.

Psychologist Philip Zimbardo explains it as a belief about whether the outcomes of our actions are contingent on what we do (internal control orientation) or on events outside our personal control (external control orientation).

This framework helps us understand how we perceive our own agency in a world that often feels unpredictable or chaotic. For instance, people with an internal locus of control tend to believe their actions directly influence outcomes, while those with an external locus of control might attribute their circumstances to external forces, such as luck, fate or the actions of others.

Recognising and shifting our locus of control, particularly towards an internal focus, can be a powerful tool in reclaiming our personal power, especially when dealing with stress, uncertainty or difficult situations. By focusing on what we can control, we regain agency and avoid the helplessness that comes with feeling at the mercy of external circumstances.

Our locus of control is not just about external circumstances but also about how we manage our internal experiences—our 'bodies', actions and responses.

The physical body

The physical body plays a foundational role in how we experience life. If we're constantly fatigued or neglecting our health, it's harder to maintain emotional balance or mental clarity. Paying attention to how we feel physically—whether it's taking time to rest, eat nourishing food, or exercise—can greatly impact how well we cope with stress and other challenges.

The emotional body

How we react to minor inconveniences, how quickly we recover from negative emotions, and how well we regulate our own emotional state are all within our control. Recognising when emotions are taking over and finding ways to regain composure—whether through deep breathing, reflection or talking things out—gives us a sense of control over our internal environment.

The mental body

When we're mentally foggy or overwhelmed, it can feel like we're not performing at our best. But by cultivating habits that improve mental clarity, like organisation, prioritisation or mindfulness, we can significantly boost our focus and confidence. Confidence comes from knowing that we are capable of managing both the mundane and the complex.

Building mental resilience doesn't mean eliminating all negative thoughts but rather learning how to manage them effectively and staying grounded in the face of uncertainty.

The spiritual body

This does not have to be religious practice, though this often guides how we experience spirituality. It simply connects us to our sense of purpose through our internal values and morality. Our spirit is what connects us to something beyond ourselves, it can offer profound strength and guidance.

Whether through religious practice, spirituality, meditation or simply moments of quiet reflection, nurturing this aspect of ourselves helps us regain perspective and calm amidst the pressures of life.

Our actions

How we behave and how we choose to respond to circumstances directly impacts the course of events in our lives. We are always making choices—whether we realise it or not.

Small actions, like taking a break when we're overwhelmed or reaching out for help when we need it, can make all the difference in how we manage stress and maintain balance. By taking ownership of our behaviours, we ensure we are responding intentionally, rather than reacting out of habit or fear.

This might involve simply 'filling our cup' by setting aside time for self-care, whether it's engaging in a hobby, resting or practicing mindfulness. Even when we're overwhelmed, making small, conscious decisions about how we engage with the world keeps us in the driver's seat of our lives.

An essential part of self-care is also knowing when to speak up— whether that's sharing what's going on with someone else or seeking support when it's needed. Often, we try to carry burdens on our own, but reaching out for help is an empowering way to retain control over our lives.

Asking for support doesn't mean we're weak or incapable; rather, it's a way to ensure we're operating at our best and protecting our well-being.

Sphere of influence

In addition to the aspects of our lives that we control directly, we have areas of influence. These are the people that we interact with regularly, where we can influence the choices someone else makes to change a set of circumstances.

While we can't control the behaviour of others, we do have the power to influence how we interact with them and how we set boundaries. For example, in personal relationships—whether with friends, family or a partner—how we communicate and set expectations impacts the dynamic.

With colleagues and importantly for us, our executives, it's similar: being clear about our needs, boundaries and capacity helps ensure mutual respect and understanding. Healthy, open communication allows us to navigate professional relationships while maintaining our sense of self.

External locus of control

However difficult it may be to accept sometimes, there are still areas outside of our control. Recognising these can help us avoid unnecessary stress. We cannot control the behaviour or feelings of others, nor can we directly control the core functions of our roles in certain situations.

These external factors are part of life, and while we can influence them to some degree, we must acknowledge the limitations of our power. For example, we may not be able to control the actions of others at work, but we can control how we respond. Likewise, we can't always control the demands placed on us, but we can manage how we approach them.

By understanding the scope of our control, influence and what lies beyond our reach, we can approach challenges with greater clarity and confidence. Shifting our focus toward what we can control—our actions, our emotions and our responses—enables us to navigate life with intention. This awareness allows us to engage more meaningfully with the world around us, ensuring that we aren't overwhelmed by external circumstances.

Instead, we empower ourselves by focusing on what we can shape, change and influence. Ultimately, embracing a strong internal locus of control fosters a sense of agency, resilience and balance, making it possible to face challenges without compromising our well-being.

Cultivating a strong internal locus of control

To cultivate a strong internal locus of control, it's essential for EAs to recognise that the real power lies in how they respond to their work environment, not in trying to manage or alter external factors beyond their reach.

Focusing on what you can control—your actions, responses and decisions—provides a solid foundation for maintaining well-being, preserving boundaries and navigating the pressures of the role with confidence.

Let's explore specific techniques EAs can incorporate into their daily routine to strengthen their internal locus of control.

1. **Mindful time management**
   One of the most direct ways to empower yourself is through managing your time with intention. This involves setting realistic expectations for the day ahead, prioritising key tasks, and implementing time-blocking techniques to ensure you have dedicated space for your work and personal life. By having clear boundaries around when you're available or off-limits, you prevent the overwhelming flood of last-minute requests or urgent tasks from taking over.
2. **Self-awareness and reflection**
   Developing self-awareness is crucial to recognising when your

boundaries are being tested or when you're starting to feel overwhelmed. Regularly check in with yourself throughout the day to assess your energy, mood and mental clarity. If you notice signs of burnout or stress, pause for a moment to recalibrate. Journaling, even for just a few minutes, can help you reflect on how you're feeling and what might need to change in your routine or mindset. By regularly tuning in to your internal state, you can more effectively manage your responses to external pressures.

3. **Emotional regulation techniques**

    In a high-stress environment, EAs often face emotionally charged situations, whether it's dealing with a demanding executive or managing competing priorities. Learning how to regulate your emotions is vital to maintaining your internal locus of control. Simple strategies like deep breathing, grounding exercises or taking a short walk to clear your mind can help you regain composure in moments of tension. By controlling how you react to challenging emotions, you preserve your mental energy and prevent burnout from taking hold.

4. **Proactive communication**

    Clear, assertive communication is one of the most powerful tools for reinforcing your boundaries and taking charge of your work environment. This means being proactive in communicating expectations and limitations, especially when it comes to your time, workload or after-hours availability. For instance, if you're feeling overwhelmed with a particular project or upcoming deadlines, openly communicating this with your executive or team helps set realistic boundaries and prevents the accumulation of unmet expectations. Addressing issues before they snowball gives you greater control over your schedule and workload, reducing stress and promoting a sense of agency.

5. **Regularly assessing priorities**

    EAs are often juggling multiple tasks and requests from various stakeholders. To maintain control over your day, it's essential to regularly reassess your priorities. At the start of each day, review your to-do list and ensure that you're focused on the most important tasks first. By consciously deciding what deserves your attention, you avoid the trap of reacting to everything in real time. This technique helps you take ownership of your time and ensures that you're investing your energy in the areas that align with your professional goals and personal well-being.

6. **Setting micro-goals and celebrating wins**
   Setting small, manageable goals helps foster a sense of accomplishment throughout the day. These micro-goals could be as simple as completing a particular task or following up on a critical project. Breaking larger objectives into bite-sized steps makes them feel more achievable and keeps you motivated. Additionally, take the time to celebrate small victories, whether that's finishing a task, handling a challenging situation, or maintaining a boundary. Recognising and acknowledging your progress helps reinforce your internal locus of control by reminding you that you are in charge of your outcomes.

7. **Building a support system**
   While EAs are often seen as the backbone of their executive's operations, it's equally important to recognise that your well-being is tied to a support network. Whether it's your colleagues, mentors or family, having trusted individuals to talk to provides a sense of shared responsibility and encouragement. When you encounter difficult situations, whether personal or professional, seeking advice or simply venting to a supportive peer can restore your sense of control. This sense of community offers both emotional reinforcement and practical strategies for managing your role.

8. **Establishing healthy routines**
   Maintaining an internal locus of control also involves taking care of your body. Establishing a healthy routine that incorporates exercise, proper nutrition and adequate sleep can significantly impact your physical and emotional resilience. When you invest in your health, you're better equipped to handle stress, remain

focused and make sound decisions. This consistency in self-care fosters greater control over your energy levels and helps you sustain your performance, even during particularly demanding periods.

9. **Using mindfulness practices**

   Mindfulness offers a powerful tool for staying grounded and maintaining control over your mental state. By practicing mindfulness techniques, such as meditation, body scans or simply paying attention to your breathing throughout the day, you can build resilience against stress and anxiety. These practices allow you to become more present in each moment, helping you focus on what you can control and release the rest.

By intentionally incorporating these strategies into your daily routine, you create an environment where your locus of control is strengthened, and your well-being is safeguarded. As an EA, taking ownership of your responses, workload and personal care helps you maintain healthy boundaries and fosters a more fulfilling, productive work life.

By maintaining focus on your locus of control, you can also reduce stress and protect your well-being. Rather than engaging in a battle over other people's behaviours, which is often beyond your control, you can concentrate on how you manage your time, energy and mental resources.

For instance, when you feel that your work–life balance is slipping, you can implement strategies like time-blocking, prioritisation or delegation to safeguard your time. These practices allow you to control the way you structure your day and how you choose to engage with tasks or projects, creating a buffer between you and the potential overwhelm of an unmanageable workload.

At the same time, boundaries are not about rigidly controlling what others do but about maintaining your personal limits with clarity and confidence. It's about understanding what you need to function at your best and communicating that effectively.

When boundaries are respected, you create an environment where you can thrive—not just as an EA but as a person. By setting boundaries that are realistic, consistent and centred around self-care, you ensure that you can continue to perform at your highest level without sacrificing your mental and physical health.

In the long term, this approach not only allows you to manage your workload but also creates a healthier, more sustainable work environment. When you focus on controlling what you can—your own actions, your own responses, your own self-care—you make space for a partnership built on mutual respect and understanding.

This leads to a more fulfilling, balanced and productive work life, where you can continue to contribute effectively while protecting the well-being that allows you to do so.

Feeding the locus of control

For us, understanding and embracing our locus of control is key to maintaining a sense of empowerment and balance in our professional and personal lives.

In any interdependent partnership, like the one you are building with your executive, it's essential for both parties to take responsibility for their actions, decisions and well-being. This shared sense of ownership fosters mutual respect, accountability and collaboration, creating a working relationship that thrives on clarity and understanding.

For EAs, recognising and feeding your locus of control means being attuned to when you need to set boundaries, seek support or push back. It involves taking proactive steps to protect your time and energy, rather than waiting for external validation or permission to assert your needs.

Once you begin to understand that many aspects of your well-being are largely within your own control, you can approach challenges with greater confidence and consistency. This might mean communicating your needs clearly, whether it's about workload management, after-hours expectations, or the level of urgency of requests. It could also mean recognising when your workload is starting to become overwhelming and advocating for support before it becomes an issue.

It's about cultivating a mindset where personal agency and boundaries are prioritised as part of the work environment, rather than merely reacting to demands as they come.

Being clear, consistent and assertive in setting boundaries ensures that EAs are not compromising our well-being for the sake of others' expectations. It also helps establish a culture of respect and understanding with your executive.

By openly communicating your needs and advocating for yourself, you can maintain a healthy work–life balance and contribute to a more sustainable work dynamic.

Ultimately, when EAs embrace their ability to control their own responses, workload and boundaries, they not only safeguard their productivity and energy but also model behaviour that promotes mutual respect and collaborative success more broadly in their work areas and other circles.

PART 2

What to do if it happens to you

CHAPTER 4
Finding the source

Burnout is a gradual process that sneaks up on us when we're constantly running on empty, unable to recharge because we're overwhelmed by a mounting pile of tasks, responsibilities and emotions.

For EAs, burnout can feel especially intense due to the pressure of supporting busy executives, managing complex schedules and juggling competing priorities. In these situations, identifying the tasks that are adding to the overwhelm is a crucial first step in preventing burnout. Understanding where the stress is coming from helps us take action before it spirals into full-blown exhaustion.

The first part of managing burnout is to identify the tasks that are consuming our time and energy without yielding meaningful results. These are often the tasks that feel overwhelming because we haven't yet sorted them out or recognised how they fit into our overall priorities.

Once we identify these tasks, we can begin to break them down and organise them in ways that reduce their emotional charge and help us see the bigger picture. This is where techniques to organise your thoughts and tasks become invaluable.

One of the simplest yet most effective ways to release mental clutter is through a 'brain dump'. This process involves writing down everything that's on your mind—tasks, worries, reminders and ideas. By putting everything on paper, you externalise your thoughts, allowing you to see the full scope of your responsibilities and identify the most pressing issues. This technique helps to reduce the mental load and free up cognitive energy, making it easier to prioritise and act.

Below is an example of a brain dump template that includes a built-in system for organising your tasks. This kind of structure is sometimes called a "parking lot". It serves as a single place to capture and manage all your to-dos, reminders and mental clutter. It's a helpful way to create mental space without worrying you'll forget something important.

That said, it doesn't need to be this detailed right away. The key is to start somewhere. A brain dump doesn't have to be pretty or perfect, it just needs to get the swirling thoughts out of your head and into a form you can work with. Whether you prefer bullet points, colour-coded lists, scribbles on a notepad, or talking it out into a voice note, the method you choose is the one that works best for you.

Think of it as expanding the storage capacity of your brain: by externalising your thoughts, you make room for focus, creativity and clarity. Over time, you can develop a system to sort and action your brain dump, but in the beginning, simply getting things out of your head is a powerful first step.

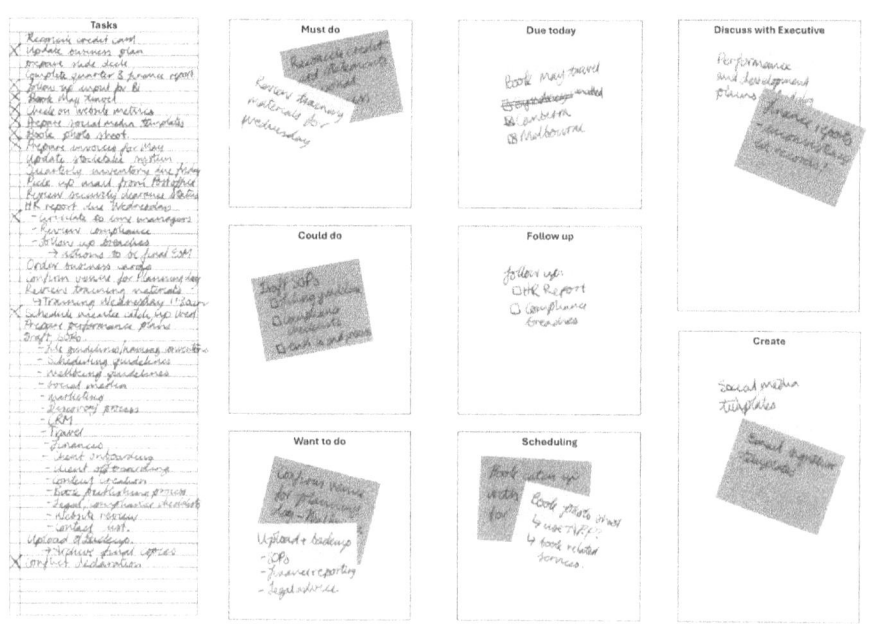

Once the brain dump is done, in whatever form works best for your brain, you can begin organising your tasks.

One of the most useful and popular tools for doing this is an Eisenhower Matrix. This method helps you distinguish between what's urgent and important, what can be delegated, and what can be deferred.

It's a simple yet effective way to filter out non-essential tasks that might be contributing to the sense of overwhelm. Tasks that are urgent but not important can often be delegated or even postponed, while the important but non-urgent tasks can be scheduled thoughtfully to prevent them from piling up.

	Urgent	Not Urgent
Important	**Do** Do these next	**Decide** Schedule a time you can do this
Not Important	**Delegate** Who is the right person to do this	**Delete** Remove unnecessary tasks

Another classic tool to tackle burnout is creating lists. While it may seem basic, lists can provide a sense of control and accomplishment for some people.

When lists become part of the problem

Many of us live by our To-Do List. To-Do Lists, action items, follow ups – they help us stay organised and focused in a fast-paced, high-demand office, but when we are facing burnout, these tools can begin to feel less like a lifeline and more like shackles. Instead of offering clarity and a path forward they can become an overwhelming reminder of everything we haven't done, adding to the mental and emotional exhaustion we are already feeling.

One of the biggest challenges we face as EAs with burnout is the sense of never 'catching up' and long ever-growing lists only feed that feeling. When our minds and bodies are already depleted, these lists can begin to trigger anxiety and guilt, making it even harder to focus or prioritise effectively. The pressure to tick things off can lead us to work from a place of urgency rather than strategy, which ultimately impacts the quality of the support we provide and further degrades our wellbeing.

As we are recovering from burnout, a critical step is to take a step back and rethink how we manage our workloads. Taking these simplified approaches to To-Do lists creates space for recovery. They help you regain that sense of control and balance, making room for rest and reflection, both of which are essential to showing up as your best self. Sometimes stepping away is the first step towards feeling whole again.

Prioritise your list according to deadlines or importance and remember that it's okay to tackle one task at a time, focusing your attention on completing the most important items first.

Alternatives

In addition to lists, using planners can provide structure to your day. A planner can be an invaluable resource for time management, helping you map out your day or week in a way that balances your professional responsibilities with personal self-care.

Planning your day in advance gives you a clear roadmap for what needs to be done and when, so you don't have to waste time deciding what to tackle next. It's not about filling every minute with work but ensuring that you allocate time for recovery and rest as well.

By organising your tasks in a way that feels manageable and clear, you begin to regain control over your workload. It allows you to approach your responsibilities with a sense of purpose, making it easier to prioritise what really matters and setting boundaries around tasks that don't align with your current goals.

When we have a plan and structure, it helps us feel grounded and capable of managing our time and energy effectively, reducing the overwhelm that can lead to burnout.

It's important to recognise that these techniques are tools, not cures. While organising tasks is an essential part of managing workload, preventing burnout requires a more holistic approach that includes setting boundaries, practicing self-care and recognising when to ask for support.

It's a combination of recognising the tasks that contribute to overwhelm and creating space for yourself, so that you can show up as your best self, both in your role and in your personal life. With the right strategies in place, you can protect your well-being and avoid the burnout that often comes from overextending yourself without sufficient recovery time.

CHAPTER 5
Finding solutions

You should now have a fairly good idea of the source of the problem. Now you can start working on what happens next. And proactively finding solutions before things spiral completely out of control.

Consider your ideal solution

When you're faced with burnout symptoms, almost everything can feel overwhelming.

When considering an approach to recovery, it's crucial to step back and consider your ideal solution. It's easy to get caught up in the immediate pressure to act or respond, especially when the demands on your time and energy are high. But taking a moment to clarify what you want the outcome to be can make a significant difference in how you approach the problem and the actions you take to resolve it.

Understanding what you want the outcome to be is the first step in this process. When you have a clear picture of your ideal solution, you can begin to make small but intentional choices that move you closer to that goal.

It's like having a destination in mind when you set out on a journey — you're more likely to reach your destination if you know where you're going. Whether it's negotiating a deadline, setting a boundary, or finding a way to balance competing priorities, knowing what you want allows you to communicate more effectively, make decisions with confidence, and stay focused on what matters most.

However, it is important to recognise that ideal solutions don't always align with the reality we find ourselves in. The nature of the workplace, the role of an EA — and life in general — is that not everything is within our control, and situations often involve multiple stakeholders with differing needs and perspectives.

You might not always be able to achieve your ideal outcome, and this is where your negotiation and compromise skills come into play. Instead of viewing these moments as a failure to achieve perfection, consider them as an opportunity to find a middle ground that still serves your needs while being realistic about what's possible.

Negotiation doesn't mean you have to give up everything you want; rather, it's about finding a balanced approach that addresses the most important aspects of your ideal solution while considering the constraints of the situation.

This process often requires open communication, flexibility and a willingness to engage with the other party to arrive at a solution that works for both sides. It's a skill that can be honed over time and is especially important in professional environments where collaboration is key.

In many cases, by negotiating effectively, you can still create an outcome that feels fair, manageable and aligned with your priorities.

Mutually beneficial solutions

While you're considering your ideal solution and recognising the potential need for negotiation, it's also valuable to look at the broader context.

How does this solution benefit not only you but also the business or the team you're part of?

What does your solution contribute to the effective development of a strong EA–executive partnership?

Taking a step back and considering the bigger picture helps you align your personal goals with the collective needs of the organisation, and the individual needs of your executives. Often, the best solutions are those that create a win-win scenario, where your needs are met without compromising the success of the business.

For example, let's say you're negotiating a deadline with your executive. Your ideal solution might involve extending the deadline to reduce your workload and ensure the quality of your work. But at the same time, you need to consider the impact on the project's timeline, the expectations of other teams, or the stakeholder's needs.

By framing the conversation in terms of how a compromise can lead to better results for everyone — such as giving you the time to produce your best work, which ultimately benefits the company's reputation — you're presenting a solution that's not only in your best interest but also in the best interest of the business.

When you think beyond your own needs, you demonstrate a collaborative, strategic mindset, which strengthens your position and builds mutual respect with others.

The process of considering your ideal solution — understanding your desires, being prepared to negotiate, and framing the benefits within the broader context of the organisation — empowers you to approach challenges thoughtfully and strategically.

It shifts the focus from feeling like a passive participant in a situation to becoming an active problem-solver who advocates for both personal well-being and organisational success. This dual focus ensures that you're not just making decisions that serve you in the moment, but that also contribute to long-term success and harmony within the workplace.

In the end, the most effective solutions often require compromise and flexibility, but that doesn't mean you're sacrificing your needs or goals.

By clearly defining what you want, engaging in productive negotiation, and considering the broader benefits, you can create outcomes that work for you and for the organisation, leading to more sustainable and fulfilling solutions.

Self-management

Self-management is at the core of maintaining a balanced and productive workday, especially for people working in high-demand roles like Executive Assistants.

Building structural supports into your day helps you not only stay organised but also safeguards your energy and well-being. The more intentional you are about managing your time, tasks and mental load, the more you set yourself up for success.

Without these structural supports, the workday can quickly become chaotic, overwhelming and exhausting. But by using strategies like brain dump templates, time blocking and bullet journaling, you can create a rhythm to your day that keeps everything running smoothly and allows you to stay in control of your workload.

Similar to a brain dump for narrowing down the triggers for your stress, one of the most effective ways to manage mental clutter and regain a sense of control is by using another brain dump that gets all of your thoughts, tasks and ideas out of your head and onto paper. Both work and non-work. This could include reminders, worries, upcoming deadlines or ideas for projects.

When everything is written down, it frees up mental space, helping you focus more clearly on the tasks at hand.

Think of this like a parking lot for intrusive and distracting thoughts. A brain dump is particularly useful in moments when you feel mentally overwhelmed or scattered. When your mind is full of things to do and you are bouncing between tasks without completing them, the act of writing everything down in one place that you can come back to helps give you clarity and direction.

By organising this brain dump into categories and priorities, you can then focus on what really needs your attention. For example, you might categorise your tasks by urgency, importance or the amount of time they require.

Once the brain dump is sorted, you'll be able to identify what tasks can be delegated, what can wait, and what needs immediate action. This process helps you prioritise effectively and ensures that no task falls through the cracks.

Another highly effective self-management strategy is time blocking. Time blocking is the practice of scheduling your day into distinct chunks of time, each dedicated to a specific task or activity.

You may already be implementing this for your executives, so why not apply the same principles to your own work? Time blocking can be especially valuable for EAs, whose responsibilities often vary from day to day.

By implementing basic time blocking techniques you can bring structure and intentionality to the day's workload. By setting aside focused blocks of time for specific activities — whether that's answering emails, preparing reports or managing schedules — you can minimise distractions and increase your productivity.

For example, if you know you have a major project to complete or a series of back-to-back meetings, you can reserve uninterrupted blocks of time in your schedule to focus on the most important tasks.

Time blocking helps you protect time for deep work, where you can fully concentrate without being interrupted. It also helps you create a sense of balance by allocating time for personal breaks, meetings and administrative tasks. With time blocking, you can feel more in control of your day, knowing exactly when you're working on specific tasks and when you can step away to recharge.

A third self-management tool to consider is bullet journaling. Bullet journaling is described by the founder of the method, Ryder Carroll, as 'a mindfulness practice that works like a productivity system'.

It is a customisable, creative method for tracking tasks, goals and progress in an organised yet flexible format. At its core, a bullet journal is a system for making lists, tracking habits, and organising your thoughts. The 'What'. And it is a way to engage with your day in a more reflective and mindful way. The 'Why'.

Bullet journaling allows you to visually track your progress and make adjustments to your workflow as needed. The beauty of a bullet journal lies in its flexibility — it's a tool that can be adapted to your unique needs, helping you keep track of daily tasks, while also providing space for creativity and self-expression.

With a bullet journal, you can create a daily or weekly log that helps you see what's on your plate, what's already been accomplished, and what still needs to be done. You can include sections for important reminders, habit tracking and even personal reflections.

By integrating both personal and professional tasks into one journal, you gain clarity and a sense of accomplishment as you check things off your list. The act of physically writing tasks down and tracking your progress can be incredibly satisfying, reinforcing your development and helping you stay motivated.

Integrating brain dumps, time blocking and bullet journaling into your day creates a framework for self-management that allows you to stay organised, reduce stress and maintain a healthy work–life balance.

These structural supports don't just help with the task at hand — they also allow you to take ownership of your time and your well-being. You can decide what gets prioritised, when to take breaks and when it's time to ask for support. With these tools in place, you'll find that not only do you accomplish more, but you also preserve the energy and focus needed to keep performing at your best.

Self-management isn't about being rigid or overly structured; it's about creating space for flexibility within a system that supports your goals and personal needs. By building these supports into your day, you set yourself up for sustainable success, knowing that you have the tools to manage your workload, protect your time and maintain your well-being.

Productivity breaks

It is really easy to get caught up in the idea that being always 'on' equates to being productive but, in reality, the opposite is true. Taking intentional breaks from work and productivity isn't a luxury but a necessity for maintaining focus, creativity and efficiency.

When we push through a work day without pausing our concentration starts to slip, decision making becomes harder and the quality of our work can suffer. When you are already struggling with similar burnout symptoms this can be catastrophic not only for your well-being but also for your work.

A short mindful break every hour or so, even just 5 or 10 minutes, gives our brains the reset they need. Taking a couple of minutes deliberately step away from your screens, take a walk, do a quick meditation or breathing exercise, or even just doing some quick stretches at your desk can help lower stress and improve your overall clarity. These moments of rest aren't lost time, they are an investment in sustained performance.

Quick Exercise:
Change your focus distance
Time required: less than 5 minutes
Frequency: At least once per hour

- Leave your desk and head to the nearest window. Look at the furthest thing you can see, pick a point and keep your eyes focused on that point for at least 20 seconds.
- Pick a point about halfway between the last point and where you are standing and focus your attention there for another 20 seconds.
- Close your eyes for 20 seconds and take a few deep breaths. Have a drink of water or make a cup of tea before getting stuck back in.

As EAs we are experts at prioritising others' needs, but not always great at remembering that we can only support others effectively when we take care of ourselves. Part of doing that is giving our minds and bodies a break.

Supported management

While you can manage burnout yourself without bothering anyone else, sometimes it sneaks up on us and gets bigger than we can manage on our own.

One of the most important ways to manage burnout effectively is through open communication with your executive. However, having these conversations can be difficult, particularly when you're feeling overwhelmed. The exhaustion and stress caused by burnout can make it hard to focus, retain information or advocate for your needs in the moment.

Managing burnout in partnership with your executive is a delicate balance, but it is possible with open communication, mutual understanding and clear boundaries.

The first step is acknowledging that burnout is a real, complex issue that requires both self-awareness and collaboration.

You don't have to navigate burnout recovery alone. By being proactive and transparent with your executive, you can create a supportive environment where both of you are invested in finding solutions.

The foundation of this partnership starts with honest and compassionate communication. It's crucial to explain what you're experiencing without fear of judgement or reprisal. When you share your challenges with your executive, focus on how burnout is impacting your ability to perform effectively.

Emphasise that this is not a reflection of your commitment or capability, but rather a result of prolonged stress and overwhelm. When your executive understands the gravity of the situation, they are more likely to be supportive and willing to help find solutions that benefit both your well-being and the success of the team.

Work together to identify areas where expectations can be adjusted or redistributed. As an EA, you may have the instinct to take on everything and ensure that everything runs smoothly, but burnout can make this unsustainable.

Have a conversation about what tasks can be delegated, what responsibilities might need to be restructured, or what priorities could be shifted.

Make it clear that you're not shirking your responsibilities but seeking to improve efficiency and focus, so that you can perform at your best.

Be clear about what you need from your executive to help alleviate the strain—whether it's additional support, a more balanced workload, or flexibility in your schedule. It's important that both of you are on the same page when it comes to finding tangible, practical solutions.

At the same time, create a system of regular check-ins. This keeps the lines of communication open and ensures that burnout doesn't sneak up on either of you.

Having a designated time to review workload, discuss well-being, and adjust plans as needed allows for a continuous feedback loop. You don't have to wait until you're at breaking point to address the issue; regular conversations will allow you to catch things early and make necessary adjustments before burnout escalates.

Finally, remember that it's about partnership. Just as you support your executive in their role, they must also support you in yours.

If your executive sees burnout as an issue that impacts both you and the team's success, they will be more inclined to make changes.

It's not just about reducing your workload but about creating an environment where both you and your executive can thrive together. Healthy collaboration and mutual support will not only help manage burnout but will also strengthen your relationship, making it more resilient in the face of future challenges.

CHAPTER 6
Framing the conversation

When you're addressing burnout with your executive, how you frame the conversation can have a significant impact on the outcome. Approaching it in a thoughtful and strategic way helps ensure the conversation is productive, respectful, and sets the stage for actionable change.

The way you present the situation—whether you're in a positive working relationship or struggling—will shape the response you receive.

Let's explore how you can effectively navigate this conversation, keeping the focus on finding solutions that benefit both you and your executive.

First and foremost, it's crucial to be open and honest about the burnout you're experiencing. Admitting to burnout can be uncomfortable, especially if you're someone who takes pride in managing a heavy workload. However, acknowledging the situation directly is the first step toward making meaningful changes.

You don't need to frame it as a personal failure or weakness; instead, it's simply a result of the demands of the role and the natural human limits on energy and focus. By presenting it this way, you create a context that is focused on problem-solving rather than blame.

When discussing the burnout, it's important to not only highlight the challenges you're facing but also emphasise the benefits of your proposed solution.

Be clear about how addressing your burnout will not only improve your well-being but also the productivity and success of the team, and ultimately, your executive's goals. For example, you could explain that adjusting your workload or setting clearer boundaries will help you bring your best self to the job, thereby improving your efficiency and focus.

By framing the conversation this way, you help your executive understand that supporting you isn't just a gesture of goodwill—it's an investment in the overall effectiveness of the team.

When your EA–executive relationship is positive

If you have cultivated a generally positive and supportive working relationship with your executive and it hasn't started to degrade due to the impact of burnout, you have a bit more leeway in how you approach the conversation.

The key here is to keep the tone casual and constructive. Rather than having a formal meeting with all the weight of a serious intervention, you can frame the conversation more as a check-in. This allows for an open exchange of thoughts, and since there's already a foundation of trust and mutual respect, you can focus on finding solutions together.

Supporting the conversation with data helps ground your concerns in objective facts. For example, you could present examples of how your workload has changed over time or offer specific data showing that your energy levels are affecting your ability to meet deadlines or perform at your usual level.

This helps to demonstrate that your experience is not just based on subjective feelings but is tied to real, measurable factors.

After having the conversation, it's important to follow up with documentation—whether private or shared with your executive.

While the conversation itself may have been informal, putting it in writing ensures that both parties are clear on what was discussed and what actions are being agreed upon. This helps prevent misunderstandings and provides a reference point if you need to revisit the issue later.

Even in a positive relationship, documentation is essential to keeping everyone on the same page and accountable.

When your EA–executive relationship is not positive

If your relationship with your executive isn't positive or is strained in any way, the approach needs to be more formal and structured. In this case, you should prepare a more data-heavy conversation to ensure that your concerns are taken seriously.

Your organisation may have an official process, but here we will cover a general approach.

Without the benefit of a warm, supportive dynamic, it's crucial to present a well-documented case that illustrates the severity of the burnout you're experiencing. This could include specific examples of the impact your symptoms are having on your work, changes in performance, or signs you have noticed of physical and emotional exhaustion.

The goal is to remove any ambiguity and clearly show how the current situation is impacting both your well-being and your work.

This activity opens you up a vulnerability if the dynamic you are working in is toxic. You may wish to slightly adjust the language you use to focus on the personal impact if you are concerned that your executive may use your disclosure as ammunition against you.

Documenting everything is especially important in situations where the relationship is less than ideal. If the conversation doesn't go well or if there's resistance to your concerns, you'll have a written record that can be referred to later.

This documentation serves as your backup, providing evidence of the discussion and what was agreed upon. Without it, it becomes easy for misunderstandings or miscommunications to occur, which can further exacerbate the issue, and cause further damage to the partnership.

Additionally, if you feel that the conversation is not being heard or if the situation doesn't improve after your discussion, your documentation can help you escalate the issue to the appropriate channels, such as Human Resources (HR) or a higher-level manager.

While this should be a last resort, due to the stress and overwhelm the official process itself can cause, having a record of your attempts to address the issue in a professional and constructive manner ensures that you've taken all reasonable steps before seeking external intervention.

If the relationship between you and your executive has degenerated beyond the point where you think a verbal conversation would be helpful or productive, you may prefer to write a detailed email notifying them of the symptoms you are experiencing, the impact it is having on your work, and what you are able to commit to, to begin resolving the issue.

You may also want to copy your HR team or approach them separately to seek support.

The power of documentation in both scenarios

Regardless of whether your relationship with your executive is positive or not, documentation plays a critical role. It acts as a safeguard, providing clarity and ensuring that both parties are held accountable to the actions and commitments made during the conversation.

In a positive relationship, documentation serves as a useful reference to help you both stay aligned on your agreed-upon next steps.

In more challenging relationships, it serves as evidence of your concerns and can be instrumental in helping you take further steps to address the issue.

In the end, the way you frame the conversation — and the actions you take before, during and after — can significantly impact the resolution of burnout.

Being open and honest, backed by data and clear communication, helps create an environment where you and your executive can work together to address the issue and ultimately create a more sustainable and balanced working relationship.

CHAPTER 7
Documentation

Why documenting conversations is essential

When you're experiencing burnout, the mental and emotional strain can make it difficult to process everything discussed in a meeting. You may leave a conversation feeling like you've agreed to certain actions but not have a clear recollection of all the details.

Burnout can cloud your ability to retain information, and this is where having a written record can be invaluable. Taking notes during the discussion you have with your executive about burnout allows you to track what was said and ensures you don't miss any important points.

In addition to helping with memory, having a documented record gives you something concrete to refer to when you need it. For example, if there's a particular change in your workload or a new approach to your responsibilities that was agreed upon, you can look back at the documentation to make sure you're on the same page.

If, over time, you feel that the agreed-upon actions aren't working or the burnout symptoms persist, you now have a detailed history to refer to. This documentation helps you assess whether the adjustments have been effective and informs the next steps in your ongoing conversations.

Another critical aspect of documentation is that it provides a baseline for future discussions.

If burnout is not improving or even intensifies, you'll have a clear reference point to see how far you've come and what might need to change.

This record serves as a roadmap to guide your next conversations with your executive, ensuring that everyone involved understands where things stand and what has been tried.

How to document conversations effectively

When it comes to documenting these important conversations, there are different methods to consider, depending on your preferences and your organisation's guidelines. The goal is to create a record that is both accurate and helpful, without being too time-consuming.

Here are some strategies to consider:

- **Recording or transcribing conversations**: If your organisation permits, one of the simplest ways to document conversations is to record or transcribe the meeting. This allows you to focus on the conversation without having to worry about taking notes during the discussion. Afterward, you can listen to the recording or read the transcript to capture all the key points. This method ensures that nothing gets overlooked, and it's especially helpful in conversations that are emotionally charged or dense with information. Of course, it's important to ensure that both you and your executive are comfortable with the recording process and that it follows any internal policies.

- **Manual notetaking**: If you prefer a more traditional approach or if recording isn't possible, taking manual notes during the meeting is another option. While this allows you to be actively engaged in the conversation. It can also be challenging, especially if you're dealing with the mental fog that often accompanies burnout. If taking notes is distracting, consider asking a colleague or trusted support person to take the notes for you. The key here is to ensure the notes are clear, comprehensive and organised, so they can serve as a useful reference later.

- **Having a support person take notes**: If you're feeling mentally drained during the conversation, it might be helpful to have someone else take the notes for you. This support person should be someone you trust, ideally someone with experience in notetaking, so they can capture the main points without distracting from the conversation itself. If you go this route, make sure the notes are thorough and cover the key discussion points.

After the meeting, review the notes with your executive to ensure accuracy and clarity.

After the conversation, it's important to share the final version of the meeting notes, whether they're transcribed, handwritten or recorded, with everyone involved.

This ensures that both you and your executive are on the same page and that nothing has been misunderstood or left out. It also provides an opportunity for both parties to clarify any details or correct any discrepancies. Such transparency promotes mutual understanding and ensures that everyone is aligned as you move forward.

What to document

The content of your documentation is just as important as how you document it.

When you're discussing burnout with your executive, focus on the following areas to ensure that the conversation is both productive and actionable:

- **Symptoms of burnout**: Begin by clearly articulating the specific symptoms of burnout you're experiencing. Are you feeling emotionally drained? struggling with mental clarity or focus? experiencing physical exhaustion? By documenting these symptoms, you help create a starting point for understanding the root causes and establishing action steps to address them.
- **Actions agreed upon**: Be sure to note any specific actions that were agreed during the meeting. For example, did you agree to adjust your workload? delegate certain tasks? implement new boundaries around working hours? Having these points documented ensures that both you and your executive have a clear understanding of what changes are being made to address your burnout.
- **Timeline and follow-up**: It's also important to document any timelines or follow-up meetings that were agreed upon. If you decide to revisit the conversation in a few weeks to assess

progress, make sure that this is clearly noted. A clear timeline helps you both stay accountable and ensures that the issue of burnout doesn't get lost in the shuffle of daily tasks.
- **Emotional tone and context**: Beyond the logistics of the conversation, take note of the emotional tone. Were you able to openly express your feelings? or did you feel uncomfortable? Did your executive show empathy and a willingness to support you? Documenting the emotional aspects of the conversation helps identify any potential barriers to resolution, such as a lack of emotional understanding or support.

Using documentation to create a collaborative action plan

Documenting your conversations about burnout is about more than just taking notes—it's about creating a framework for a collaborative action plan. By putting everything in writing, both you and your executive can stay aligned on the necessary steps to address burnout.

Documentation serves as a tool for accountability, helping both parties stay committed to making meaningful changes.

This approach also empowers you as the EA. You're not simply relaying a problem to your executive; you're actively participating in the solution. You have a clear record of what's been discussed, and you are in a stronger position to advocate for your needs moving forward.

This sense of agency is important in maintaining your well-being and ensuring that you don't fall into unhealthy patterns of overwork.

Ultimately, the goal is to create a balanced partnership, where both you and your executive understand the challenges burnout presents, and work together to find sustainable solutions.

By documenting your conversations, you're building a foundation of transparency and mutual understanding. This not only helps you manage your burnout more effectively but also strengthens the overall dynamic between you and your executive, ensuring a healthier and more productive working relationship.

Navigating HR processes for escalating burnout

Burnout is a serious issue. Where internal support systems aren't enough, or aren't effective, escalating the issue to HR may be necessary. Every business has different processes but, typically, the usual process would be that the impacted person (you) would reach out to their manager (your executive) or an HR representative to express their concerns.

The next step will usually involve an assessment of your well-being and workload, where HR may engage in confidential conversations with you, your executives and sometimes other witnesses or stakeholders to better understand your circumstances.

Once burnout is identified, HR may offer support in the form of counselling, workload adjustments, workplace flexibility or potentially recommending a temporary leave of absence.

In extreme cases, where your mental health is severely impacted, they may also refer you to workers compensation. Depending on the severity, HR might also investigate the work environment, and the expectations placed on you to ensure any systemic issues are addressed.

These investigations can sometimes lead to improvements in company policies or work structures to prevent burnout.

However, it is important to remember that there can be risks when involving HR in burnout cases. While they are trained to handle such matters confidentially and professionally, there can be reputational risks around how your situation is perceived, particularly if your burnout can be linked to specific managers or teams.

You may also have concerns about your future career prospects or relationships within the business. It is important that you weigh these risks and have an open discussion with the HR team about confidentiality and the support options available to you before making any decisions.

Kathleen Harvey

PART 3

Now what?

CHAPTER 7
Deliberate healing

Deliberate healing is a proactive, intentional approach to recovering from burnout, stress or any other form of emotional or physical strain.

Unlike reactive healing, which often happens out of necessity when the body or mind can no longer keep up, deliberate healing involves actively choosing to prioritise self-care and well-being before reaching a breaking point.

It's about recognising the need for recovery and taking intentional steps to restore balance and energy, rather than waiting for burnout to force you into a state of crisis.

For EAs, deliberate healing is especially crucial.

The nature of the role is demanding, often requiring a constant juggling of priorities, emotional labour and high-stakes decision-making. The burnout that can come from such a high level of responsibility doesn't just happen overnight; it builds over time, often masked by a drive for perfection and a deep sense of responsibility.

By engaging in deliberate healing, you can take ownership of your well-being, addressing the signs of stress before they become overwhelming and setting boundaries that safeguard both your personal energy and professional performance.

One of the key components of deliberate healing is recognising the importance of rest and recovery.

In a work environment that values productivity and constant availability, taking time for rest can feel like a luxury or even a sign of weakness. But the reality is that rest is a necessity, not a reward. By making space for adequate sleep, mindful breaks throughout the day, and time off when needed, you can create the physical and mental space necessary for healing.

This doesn't mean abandoning work altogether—it simply means stepping back long enough to recharge so that you can return to it with more focus, clarity and energy.

Another crucial aspect of deliberate healing is the cultivation of mental and emotional resilience. It's easy to feel overwhelmed when juggling multiple tasks and demands, but learning to manage emotions and maintain a sense of calm in the face of chaos can make all the difference.

This might involve developing mindfulness practices, engaging in regular reflection or journaling, or seeking support from mentors, therapists or peers.

The goal is to create a toolkit of strategies that can help you manage stress and prevent it from escalating. By consciously investing in mental and emotional well-being, you not only help yourself, but also ensure that you can remain effective in your role.

It is important to remember that healing is not a one-time fix but an ongoing process. It's about consistently checking in with yourself, identifying when you're nearing your limits, and taking the necessary steps to reset before you're stretched too thin.

This might mean adjusting work hours, setting new boundaries, or simply recognising that it's okay to not be 'on' all the time.

Healing is not a destination—it's a constant ebb and flow, like the tide, which requires regular attention and care. It is through this commitment to self-maintenance that you can learn to thrive, both personally and professionally.

Healing begins the moment you make the conscious decision to break out of the pattern. For many Executive Assistants, burnout and stress are not one-time occurrences but part of a recurring cycle—a pattern of overwork, neglect of personal needs, and a persistent drive to please or take care of everyone but ourselves.

It's easy to fall into this cycle, especially in a role where the demands of the executive and the organisation can feel all-consuming. But real healing starts when you decide, with full awareness, to step off the treadmill and stop the endless cycle.

Breaking out of the pattern requires a shift in mindset — a willingness to see that continuing down the same path will only lead to more exhaustion, frustration and, ultimately, burnout. The decision to step away from the pattern is an act of self-empowerment, a declaration that your health, energy and boundaries matter.

It's about recognising that your well-being is not a luxury or a secondary consideration; it's an essential part of your ability to show up effectively for your work and your life. It's not a passive process; it's an active choice to change how you engage with both your role and yourself.

This shift often begins with small but meaningful actions — things like setting boundaries where there were none before, communicating openly about your needs, and making time for rest.

It may feel uncomfortable at first, especially if you've been conditioned to put others first and neglect your own needs. But each time you make a decision that prioritises your well-being, you're breaking the cycle, and, over time, those small shifts create a ripple effect.

The more you honour your limits, the easier it becomes to recognise when you're veering into overdrive and take steps to recalibrate before you hit the wall.

Healing also begins when you stop waiting for permission. So often, EAs look for validation from others — whether from your executive, colleagues or even the organisational culture itself — before taking care of themselves. But true healing only happens when you take ownership of your own health and well-being, acknowledging that you don't need external approval to protect your energy.

The act of reclaiming your power in this way is transformative. You break free from the pattern by owning your right to rest, to ask for help, to set boundaries, and to pursue a work–life balance that honours your humanity as much as your role.

In these moments of decision—when you choose to break the cycle and prioritise healing—you create a new pattern, one that serves not only your personal well-being but your professional performance as well.

Healing doesn't require a grand gesture; it's in the small, deliberate choices you make each day to break out of the pattern and step into a new way of being. It's these shifts, over time, that lead to lasting recovery and a more sustainable, fulfilling approach to both work and life.

Seeking professional support

Seeking professional therapy and other support is a crucial step in the healing journey, especially for Executive Assistants who often face the weight of overwhelming expectations, emotional labour, and high-pressure environments.

While self-care practices and personal strategies are valuable, sometimes the complexity of burnout, stress or emotional fatigue requires the insight, expertise and guidance of a trained professional.

It is also important to understand that therapy isn't just for times of crisis; it can be an essential resource for maintaining your mental health, processing difficult emotions, and learning the tools needed to cope with the challenges of a demanding role.

For EAs, the demands of the work often mean putting the needs of others ahead of your own. This can lead to feelings of isolation, burnout and emotional exhaustion, as you absorb not only the workload but also the emotional energy of those you support.

Therapy offers a safe, non-judgemental space to process these emotions, allowing you to explore feelings of resentment, stress or frustration in a way that is constructive and healing. Through therapy, you can gain a deeper understanding of the dynamics that contribute to burnout and work to shift the patterns that may be negatively impacting your mental and emotional health.

Therapists offer specialised tools and coping strategies that can help individuals manage the intense pressure that often comes with high-stakes environments.

Cognitive behavioural therapy (CBT), mindfulness-based practices and emotional regulation techniques are just a few examples of approaches that can be tailored to an individual's needs.

By engaging in therapy, you can learn how to reframe negative thoughts, manage anxiety, and develop healthier responses to stress. These skills can not only enhance your personal well-being but also improve job performance, as they allow you to approach your work with greater clarity, focus and resilience.

In addition to therapy, seeking other supports—such as mentorship, peer groups or employee assistance programs (EAPs)—can further bolster your ability to navigate challenging moments.

Mentors and colleagues who understand the unique pressures of your role can provide valuable advice and emotional support, offering a sense of community and shared experience.

Your network of support doesn't have to be limited to just one-on-one therapy sessions. Group therapy or peer support groups can also provide a sense of belonging and validation, reinforcing the understanding that burnout and stress are not unique to one person but are part of a shared experience.

Ultimately, seeking professional therapy and other support is an act of self-empowerment. It signals a commitment to long-term well-being, resilience and a healthier approach to work.

In the demanding world of an EA, it's easy to feel like you're alone in your struggles, but the truth is that there are resources and supports available to help navigate the challenges. By seeking help, you are investing in yourself, your future and your ability to continue excelling in your role without sacrificing your mental and emotional health.

Take meaningful breaks from work

Taking regular, meaningful breaks from work is one of the most effective strategies you can implement for preventing burnout and maintaining long-term productivity.

In a world where EAs are often tethered to their devices — responding to emails, Slack messages, Teams messages, handling urgent requests and constantly shifting between tasks — disconnecting can feel counterintuitive.

The quality of the break is far more important than its length. It's not about the number of minutes you spend away from your desk but how you use that time to recharge and reset. When you step away from your work and unplug from your work devices, you're giving your brain and body the chance to rest and recover, which ultimately leads to better focus, creativity and resilience when you return.

The key here is intentionality. A short break can be just as effective — if not more so — than a longer one, as long as you are fully present and away from the demands of work.

Checking emails or answering calls during a break defeats the purpose of disconnecting. Instead, use that time to do something restorative. Go for a walk, stretch, meditate or simply sit in silence. The goal is to step out of the work mindset and allow your nervous system to relax. Even just 10 or 15 minutes of undistracted time can make a significant difference in your ability to refocus and manage stress. It's about creating a boundary that allows you to fully reset before diving back into the next task.

Quality breaks also give you the opportunity to check in with yourself. How are you feeling? What's weighing on your mind? Are there any emotions or tensions you need to release?

Taking a break without the constant pull of work-related notifications or worries enables you to tap into what your body and mind truly need. This mindfulness, even in brief moments, is a form of self-care that can help prevent burnout from creeping up unnoticed.

Whether you use the break to nourish your body with a healthy snack or practice deep breathing to release tension, you're giving yourself the space to reset, which can improve both your well-being and your effectiveness when you return to your tasks.

When you make unplugged breaks a regular part of your routine, you build resilience against the ongoing demands of the role. It's about shifting from a reactive mindset—where you're constantly responding to the next demand—to a proactive one, where you intentionally manage your energy and capacity.

By focusing on the quality of your breaks and giving yourself the space to truly disconnect, you create a more sustainable work rhythm that allows you to perform at your best without running yourself into the ground.

The benefits are far-reaching: improved concentration, better decision-making, reduced stress and a more balanced approach to both work and life.

The role of creativity and hobbies in managing burnout

Engaging in activities that nurture our creative side can offer a refreshing break from the constant pressures of work.

Creative activities stimulate the brain in ways that can help reduce stress, increase problem solving abilities and restore a sense of balance in our lives. Whether it is painting, writing, cooking or playing music, these outlets not only allow us to unwind but also provide a sense of accomplishment outside of the workplace.

Hobbies play a critical role in preventing burnout by giving us the opportunity to fully disconnect from our work. These activities serve as a mental reset, helping us recharge and allowing us to be present in the moment.

It is important to find something that brings both fun and satisfaction, even if it is only for a couple of minutes a day. Hobbies give us the freedom to relax and recharge without the pressures of performance deadlines.

Important note: Social media is not a hobby.

While it may feel like a way to unwind, scrolling through feeds can often lead to mental fatigue and increased stress.

Social media tends to keep us engaged in a cycle of comparison and over stimulation, which can contribute to burnout rather than alleviate it.

Instead, look for activities that provide a true mental break. Something that allows you to focus on something tangible and rewarding, without the constant pull of mindless distraction.

Finding time for creativity and hobbies can help us stay grounded, boost our mental and emotional wellbeing, and ultimately enhance our work performance.

Building resilience and confidence

Building resilience and confidence in your professional capabilities is an ongoing journey, one that requires intentional effort and self-compassion.

In the fast-paced and high-pressure world we operate in as EAs, the challenges can often feel overwhelming, and moments of self-doubt are natural. However, what sets resilient professionals apart is their ability to manage these doubts and keep moving forward.

One of the most impactful ways you can cultivate resilience is through self-promotion, which often takes the form of positive self-talk. The way you speak to yourself and about yourself, can either fuel your confidence or undermine it. It's easy to focus on what you didn't do right or to downplay your accomplishments, but shifting that internal narrative is key to building lasting self-assurance.

By consciously choosing to acknowledge your strengths, skills and past successes, you're training your brain to recognise your value. Whether it's celebrating a completed project, mastering a new software tool, or managing a particularly difficult situation, recognising and affirming your achievements empowers you to keep striving toward growth.

The mindset of 'yet'

Positive self-talk is not just about giving yourself a pat on the back. It's about reframing challenges and obstacles in a way that supports your resilience. When you encounter something difficult, instead of thinking 'I can't do this', try shifting to 'I'm still learning how to do this' or 'I can't do this yet.'

This small change in language fosters a mindset where you can see your mistakes as learning opportunities rather than failures. Over time, this approach reduces the fear of taking on new challenges, allowing you to step into unfamiliar tasks with a sense of curiosity and confidence. It creates a culture within yourself where growth and progress are prioritised over perfection, enabling you to approach your work with greater ease and self-assurance.

When faced with a task that feels out of reach, instead of internalising that sense of incapability, you recognise that growth takes time. Saying 'yet' adds an important dimension to your thinking: this is a skill, a task or a challenge you haven't mastered — *yet*.

By embracing this mindset, you are acknowledging that growth is a process, not an immediate destination. This small but mighty shift in perspective opens up the possibility for learning and experimentation, removing the pressure to be perfect right away.

It also encourages a sense of patience with yourself, which is crucial when you're striving to learn new skills or navigate complex situations. Rather than being defeated by challenges, you start to see them as stepping stones that help you grow stronger and more capable.

These tactics help you create space for failure to be part of your learning journey. Instead of seeing mistakes as evidence of inadequacy, they become valuable moments of feedback.

The key to resilience lies in your ability to keep going, even when things don't go as planned. Embracing the mindset of 'yet' allows you to build confidence in your ability to adapt, learn and improve. It reminds you that no accomplishment comes without its fair share of struggles, and each time you try and fail, you're one step closer to mastering the skill or task at hand.

As you continue to practice self-promotion and the power of yet, you'll find that your resilience becomes more ingrained. You will be better equipped to handle the demands of your role, knowing that setbacks don't define your capabilities but rather shape them.

Confidence grows not just from external praise, but from an internal belief that you can tackle whatever comes your way, and that even if you don't have all the answers now, you *will* find them. In this way, resilience becomes a foundation that supports your ability to keep moving forward, navigating challenges with both grace and strength.

Building confidence and resilience at work is an ongoing process, one that thrives on consistency and intention. While positive self-talk and the power of yet are essential tools, there are other strategies that can significantly enhance your ability to stay confident and resilient in the workplace.

Embracing small wins

One of the most powerful methods is embracing small wins. In the whirlwind of daily tasks and responsibilities, it's easy to overlook the small victories that add up over time.

Whether it's successfully managing a complex calendar, resolving a tense situation with diplomacy, completing a challenging task, or even just having a quiet day, these small wins are often the building blocks of your professional growth. Celebrating these moments, no matter how seemingly insignificant, helps reinforce your sense of competence and accomplishment.

Over time, you'll begin to recognise just how much you're truly capable of, and that awareness can bolster both your confidence and resilience.

Setting realistic expectations

Another crucial aspect of building resilience is setting realistic expectations for yourself. It's common, especially for high-achieving individuals like Executive Assistants, to hold ourselves to impossibly high standards.

Constantly striving for perfection can lead to burnout and self-doubt when expectations aren't met.

Resilience comes from accepting that mistakes are part of the process and that 'good enough' is often more than sufficient. Learning to adjust your expectations — setting goals that challenge you but are still within reach — allows you to build confidence while preventing the frustration that comes with unattainable standards.

It's about finding a balance between striving for excellence and allowing yourself room to grow and make mistakes without feeling like you've failed. This mindset shift not only strengthens your ability to manage stress but also helps you maintain a healthier relationship with your work and your own performance.

Seeking feedback

Seeking feedback is another invaluable tool in building confidence. It may seem intimidating at first, but actively asking for feedback from colleagues or your executive can provide clarity on areas where you're excelling and areas that may need improvement.

This proactive approach not only helps you become more self-aware but also signals to others that you're committed to growth.

Positive feedback can serve as a powerful confidence booster, reminding you of the skills and strengths you might overlook in the hustle of day-to-day responsibilities.

Constructive criticism, on the other hand, offers valuable insight into how you can improve, helping you refine your approach and grow professionally.

By making feedback a regular part of your work routine, you foster an environment of continual learning, which enhances your resilience and keeps you focused on growth rather than perfection.

Building a support network

Finally, building a support network at work can have a profound impact on your confidence and resilience. When you surround yourself with colleagues or mentors who encourage, support and challenge you, you create an environment where both personal and professional growth can thrive.

EAs are typically a fairly approachable bunch. Developing a network of EAs in your organisation and the organisations you work closely with has a huge positive impact on both your well-being and your productivity.

Having a trusted group of people to lean on for advice or encouragement can help you navigate tough times with a sense of camaraderie and reassurance. Knowing that you're not alone in your struggles can make a world of difference, especially when faced with challenges that feel overwhelming.

This network doesn't just offer emotional support; it can also provide different perspectives and insights that help you overcome obstacles more effectively. Resilience is not only about bouncing back on your own but about recognising the strength that comes from collaboration and shared experiences.

By incorporating these strategies into your daily routine — celebrating small wins, setting realistic expectations, seeking feedback and building a support network — you create a holistic approach to building confidence and resilience.

Each of these practices feeds into the others, helping you develop a more resilient mindset that not only helps you face challenges but thrives in the face of them. With time, these habits will become second nature, empowering you to face any professional hurdle with confidence, poise and the inner strength to keep moving forward.

Building strong positive relationships

Building stronger, more supportive relationships with the executives and teams you support is essential for creating a collaborative and effective work environment.

As an Executive Assistant, you're often the linchpin that keeps everything running smoothly, and fostering strong relationships with those around you can make all the difference in not only your well-being but also the overall success of the team.

A key element in building these relationships is communication. Open, honest and transparent communication is the foundation of any strong partnership. This means not just relaying information effectively, but also actively listening to the needs and concerns of your executive and colleagues.

By making space for others to share their thoughts and feedback, you demonstrate that you value their perspectives and are committed to understanding their priorities.

One way to build positive relationships is by anticipating needs and being proactive. Executives often work under high pressure and tight deadlines, and the ability to foresee their needs before they have to ask can set you apart as a trusted partner.

This doesn't just mean managing schedules or handling logistics — it's about understanding the bigger picture and supporting your executive's goals.

For instance, if you notice a meeting is approaching and certain information is still pending, you can take the initiative to gather what's needed or remind the executive of the next steps.

Similarly, when working with teams, showing that you understand the team's collective goals and individual responsibilities helps you connect with them on a deeper level, making it easier to collaborate and support one another. This proactive approach not only builds trust but also fosters a sense of reliability and mutual respect.

Another crucial strategy is consistent follow-through. Building trust with your executive and team comes from delivering on your promises and commitments.

If you say you will handle a task, ensure you follow through, and if there's a delay or issue, communicate it early. Try not to commit to tasks or activities that will over-extend you or be difficult to achieve in the time available to you.

Consistency builds credibility, and the more dependable you are, the more confidence others will have in your abilities.

In addition to following through on tasks, it's also important to be clear about expectations. Setting up regular check-ins or status updates with your executive helps ensure that both of you are on the same page, preventing misunderstandings and giving you the opportunity to adjust priorities as needed.

Likewise, with teams, having regular touchpoints and open communication about expectations can strengthen the overall dynamic and improve collaboration.

Empathy plays a significant role in building stronger relationships as well. Taking the time to understand the pressures and challenges your executive and teammates face helps you tailor your support in a way that's both meaningful and effective.

This doesn't mean you have to solve all of their problems, but demonstrating understanding and compassion can go a long way in creating a positive work environment. By offering a listening ear, validating their concerns, or simply acknowledging their hard work, you help create a supportive culture where people feel valued.

When people feel seen and understood, they're more likely to engage positively and work together as a cohesive unit.

Lastly, mutual respect is paramount in any relationship. Respecting your executive's time, decisions and expertise while expecting the same in return fosters an environment where both parties feel valued.

For teams, respecting different work styles, preferences and boundaries promotes collaboration and reduces conflict. When you approach each relationship with respect, you set a standard for others to follow, ensuring that the work environment is one where everyone can thrive.

Building strong, supportive relationships is not about grand gestures—it's about the small, consistent actions that demonstrate care, reliability and understanding.

By focusing on clear communication, anticipating needs, following through on commitments, demonstrating empathy, and fostering mutual respect, you can create lasting and productive relationships with your executives and teams.

These connections not only make your work life smoother but also contribute to the overall success of the organisation.

CHAPTER 9
The next right step

Healing doesn't need to feel like just another task on your already overflowing to-do list. When starting the journey of recovery, it's crucial to take it slow and manageable so that the process itself doesn't inadvertently add to your overwhelm.

The idea is not to push yourself too hard or make healing another pressure-filled goal to achieve but to focus on small, intentional actions that bring comfort and relief without causing stress. Small, simple activities can be incredibly powerful, and starting small ensures that these healing practices become integrated into your routine gradually, instead of feeling like another burden.

Mindfulness

One of the most accessible ways to begin your healing process is through practicing mindfulness.

Mindfulness is about being present in the moment, without judgement or distraction. It can be as simple as taking a few deep breaths before responding to an email, focusing on the sensation of your hands on your keyboard, or even becoming aware of the temperature of the air around you.

This practice doesn't require a significant time investment or any particular space. The beauty of mindfulness is that it's flexible and can be easily incorporated into daily activities. You don't need to sit down for a structured mindfulness session to benefit from it. You can do it while commuting, having a coffee, or even during a quick break.

The key is to give yourself a few moments where you step out of autopilot mode and focus on the now, with no agenda other than being present.

When you first begin, it's important to remember that mindfulness isn't about achieving perfect calm or silencing your mind—it's about gently guiding your attention back to the present, no matter how chaotic or busy it feels. By starting small, you're creating little pauses throughout your day that can serve as grounding moments, which help reduce the overall mental and emotional load. Over time, these small moments of mindfulness build up and contribute to a sense of balance and peace, even amid a busy workday.

Meditation

To take it a step further, another tool to help you manage stress and build resilience is meditation.

Meditation is widely known for its stress-relieving benefits, but like mindfulness, it doesn't need to be overwhelming or take up a lot of time. You don't need to meditate for long stretches of time or with complicated rituals.

Simply carving out five to ten minutes each day to sit quietly and focus on your breath can work wonders for your mental health.

You don't need to be an expert in meditation to reap its rewards; apps and online resources make it easy to get started with guided meditations, many of which are designed for beginners. These can range from simple breathing exercises to more structured mindfulness practices that guide you through visualisations or body scans.

One of the key aspects of meditation is its ability to train your mind to slow down and break the cycle of constant overthinking. It provides a mental reset, offering clarity and reducing anxiety. As with mindfulness, the goal isn't necessarily to 'clear your mind', but rather to notice when your mind begins to wander and gently guide it back to your focus.

By practicing consistently, even for just a few minutes each day, you can develop a greater sense of mental clarity and calmness that will carry over into other aspects of your life, especially when stress begins to build.

Journaling

Journaling is another incredibly effective and accessible way to begin healing.

Writing down your thoughts, feelings and experiences allows you to release pent-up emotions and gain a deeper understanding of yourself. Journaling doesn't need to be an elaborate practice or require long entries — just a few minutes each day can help clarify your thoughts and provide a sense of relief.

If you're unsure where to begin, journaling prompts can serve as a helpful starting point. Simple prompts like 'What went well today?' or 'How am I feeling right now?' can help focus your thoughts and prevent overwhelm.

These questions guide you to reflect on the positive aspects of your day, no matter how small, and can shift your mindset toward gratitude and appreciation.

Alternatively, you can challenge yourself with journaling activities, like a '30-day gratitude challenge', where you write about something you're grateful for every day. 'Reflective journaling' is where you explore your thoughts and feelings more deeply.

The idea is to make journaling a gentle, consistent habit that helps you reconnect with yourself, process difficult emotions, and gain insight into how you're feeling. Over time, journaling can help you uncover patterns in your thoughts and behaviours, allowing you to identify stress triggers and develop healthier coping mechanisms.

It's a space where you don't need to be perfect, but rather, a space to let your emotions flow freely without judgement.

Creativity

Creativity plays a unique and powerful role in healing because it encourages self-expression in a less structured, more fluid way. Engaging in creative activities allows you to process emotions, release tension and reconnect with a sense of joy.

It's important to approach creativity with the understanding that it doesn't need to be about producing something perfect—it's about enjoying the process.

One easy way to start integrating creativity into your healing routine is through timed drawing challenges. These challenges are designed to encourage quick, spontaneous drawing without the pressure to create a masterpiece. For example, you can set a timer for 10 minutes and draw something that represents your current state of mind or emotions.

You don't need to be an artist to benefit from this; the goal is simply to express yourself through art in a low-pressure, time-limited way. The process of drawing helps you focus on the present moment, letting go of expectations, and engaging with your creativity in a nonjudgemental space.

These challenges can be a fun and effective way to take a break from your usual routine and provide a mental reset, while also giving you a sense of accomplishment, no matter how simple or abstract the drawing may be.

Starting small with these healing practices means you're gently easing yourself into the process without overwhelming yourself.

Whether it's a few minutes of mindfulness, a short meditation session, a quick journaling prompt, or a 10-minute creative challenge, each of these activities offers a way to recharge and refocus your mind. The key is to approach them with curiosity, self-compassion and patience. Healing is a journey, not a race, and starting small allows you to integrate these practices into your life without adding stress.

Over time, these small steps will build a foundation of well-being and resilience that supports you through the ups and downs of daily life. By making space for healing in a way that feels comfortable and manageable, you create an environment where recovery is not only possible but sustainable.

It is time to set your boundaries

As we have discussed, setting clear boundaries is an essential practice for Executive Assistants who juggle multiple tasks, priorities and the high demands of supporting an executive. In a role where you are constantly responding to requests, handling urgent matters, and managing an executive's schedule, it can be easy to lose sight of your own limits.

Boundaries are crucial for maintaining a balance between personal well-being and professional responsibilities. They're not about building walls but creating a framework where you can work effectively without sacrificing your health or mental state.

The first boundary to set with your executive is clearly defining work hours. If you've agreed that your working day ends at 6 pm, make it known that you won't be available for non-urgent requests after that time.

Or perhaps you need to set boundaries around last-minute changes to meetings or events, letting your executive know that while you're happy to be flexible, repeated last-minute changes create undue stress and compromise your ability to deliver.

Clear communication about these boundaries ensures both you and your executive understand what is reasonable, fostering a more respectful and efficient working relationship. When you set and enforce these boundaries consistently, you not only protect your time but also cultivate an environment where your role is respected.

Additionally, being clear about your emotional boundaries is just as important. As an EA, you may often be in the middle of emotional dynamics, particularly with your executive.

You might be asked to manage conflicts or absorb some of the stress and pressures your executive faces. While it's part of the job, it's essential to establish emotional boundaries to prevent burnout.

This might mean stepping back when a situation is becoming overwhelming or knowing when to pass on certain tasks to others who can better manage them.

It is also important to communicate when your emotional bandwidth is stretched so that your executive understands the importance of mutual respect for your emotional space.

Setting boundaries as an EA is a continuous process of negotiation and reassessment. As your role evolves or as your executive's demands change, your boundaries may need to be adjusted.

Regularly checking in with yourself—whether that's during weekly reflections or monthly check-ins with your executive—can help you reassess whether your boundaries are still serving you or if they need tweaking. It's also crucial to involve your executive in the process, so they're on the same page and can collaborate with you to ensure that your boundaries are respected.

Over time, consistent boundary-setting not only helps you manage workload and stress but also ensures that you remain in a position to give your best work, contributing to a stronger, more sustainable professional relationship.

Boundaries are not about controlling others; they are about protecting *yourself*. Think of them as your personal rulebook—a guide for how you expect to be treated and how you will navigate the dynamics of your relationships, both at work and in life. Healthy boundaries are crucial for ensuring that your needs are met, your well-being is maintained, and your work–life balance is respected.

These boundaries help you preserve your mental and physical energy, prevent burnout, and ensure that you're able to perform at your best without sacrificing your happiness.

The key to setting effective boundaries is remembering that they are for *you*, not for the people around you. It's easy to fall into the trap of wanting to manage the behaviour of others, but that's not where your control lies.

Instead, focus on what you are willing to tolerate and how you will respond when those limits are pushed. Setting clear, realistic expectations is an essential part of the process.

These expectations should reflect your needs, limits and priorities — be it how much work you're willing to take on, the time you're willing to commit, or the level of respect you require from those around you.

Additionally, a good boundary always comes with a consequence — a clear and respectful response if those boundaries are violated.

Importantly, the consequence must always be within your *locus of control*. You can't control how others behave, but you can control how you choose to respond when your boundaries are crossed.

Maybe the consequence is taking a break, rescheduling a meeting, or escalating an issue to ensure it gets addressed. Whatever the consequence, it should serve as a way to reinforce your limits and remind others of your expectations, without escalating conflict or compromising your well-being.

By focusing on what you can control — your own responses and actions — you can create a healthier, more respectful environment where your boundaries are respected. And remember, boundaries are a form of self-respect. They signal to others that your time, energy and well-being matter just as much as anyone else's.

Understand when to move on

Knowing when it's time to seek a new executive partnership is an incredibly difficult, yet crucial decision for any Executive Assistant.

In a role that demands trust, collaboration and mutual respect, the relationship you share with your executive is foundational to both your professional success and your well-being. However, not every executive partnership is going to be sustainable, and recognising when it's time for a change can prevent further stress and potential burnout.

A clear sign that it might be time to seek a new partnership is when your well-being is consistently compromised, despite your efforts to communicate and set boundaries.

If you've had multiple conversations with your executive about work expectations, workload management and boundaries, but there is little to no shift in behaviour, you may find yourself in a position where your needs are not being respected. If work–life balance continues to slip away, you feel undervalued or unseen, or your physical and emotional health is in jeopardy, these are major red flags that cannot be ignored.

No job or partnership is worth sacrificing your health, and continuing to tolerate an unhealthy dynamic may lead to long-term damage.

Another indicator is when your contributions are no longer appreciated or acknowledged. As an EA, you put in significant effort to keep the executive and the team functioning smoothly, often behind the scenes. If your work goes unrecognised, if you feel consistently overlooked, or if there is a lack of gratitude for your role, this can erode your sense of purpose and job satisfaction. When the partnership becomes one-sided or you're no longer empowered to use your skills in meaningful ways, it's a sign that the relationship may no longer be serving your professional growth.

Sometimes, the need to look for a new partnership comes when there's a fundamental mismatch in working styles. While no two individuals are exactly alike, a healthy EA-executive relationship is built on mutual understanding, open communication and respect.

If you find that you and your executive are fundamentally misaligned in terms of priorities, communication styles or goals, this can lead to frustration and inefficiency. Even with effort, it can become difficult to maintain a productive and harmonious working relationship if these core differences remain unresolved.

Making the decision to look for a new executive partnership is not something to take lightly, but it's also an act of self-preservation.

It's essential to prioritise your mental and emotional well-being so that you can continue to thrive in your role, whether with your current executive or in a new position. Recognising when it's time to seek change is an empowering step in ensuring that you remain in a role where you can contribute meaningfully, be respected, and ultimately grow professionally without sacrificing your personal health.

Kathleen Harvey

PART 4

Tools

CHAPTER 10
Embracing new technology to manage burnout

As EAs we often wear many hats, juggling countless responsibilities while staying two steps ahead. This constant demand for efficiency and perfection creates the perfect environment for burnout to take root and flourish.

One way we can lighten the load and safeguard our wellbeing is to seek out and embrace new technology. Using the right tools can help you to automate tasks, streamline communication and give you back some precious extra minutes that can be spent on higher impact work or self-care activities.

Technology is being designed specifically for productivity and support roles, and it is improving all the time. Tools from automated scheduling assistants to workflow automation to knowledge management systems can transform how you manage your workload.

Depending on your organisation's policies you may be able to access tools that will help you manage meetings without the back-and-forth emails, keep tasks organised and visible with project management apps, automate your credit card reconciliation process or even use AI tools to help with drafting content, correspondence or other documents.

By taking the time to research and learn how to use some of these tools you reduce the mental load of keeping track of every detail manually, allowing you to focus more on strategic support rather than administrative catch up.

These tools can be a safety net that supports your role so when burnout knocks your productivity down to next to nothing you will have something ticking away in the background to keep things on track while you get back on your feet.

By using tech to create structure and efficiency you not only become more effective with less effort but also safeguard your wellbeing. Technology is a powerful ally in delivering the vital role you play in an organisation.

Meeting management

Managing meetings can be one of the most time consuming and detail heavy tasks we manage as Executive Assistants. Fortunately, there are a wide range of tools designed to make scheduling, coordination and follow-up much more efficient, ultimately reducing stress and helping prevent burnout.

While it is important to note that technology is evolving all the time and when you are reading this there may be other tools that are better suited to your work, here are a few tools that can make a big difference:

Scheduling tools

Automate the process of finding and booking meeting times:

- **Calendly**: A self-service tool that syncs with your calendar (and your executive's calendar) and lets others choose from the available time slots. The tool is designed to prevent double booking and eliminate the majority of the back-and-forth emails about scheduling.
- **Clockwise**: An AI calendar assistant that automatically moves flexible meetings to create larger blocks of focussed work time. This is useful to maximise your Executive's availability by avoiding fragmented schedules to boost productivity.
- **Doodle**: A group polling tool ideal for coordinating meetings with multiple participants. You propose several time options and attendees vote on the best time.

Meeting management and preparation tools

Organise your agendas and other meeting papers, track decisions and manage follow ups:

- **Fellow**: A collaborative agenda and meeting note tool. It keeps everyone aligned by allowing participants to add agenda items, take shared notes and assign action items to ensure meetings stay focussed and productive.
- **Notion or OneNote**: Versatile digital workspaces where you can organise meeting materials, from agendas to notes and follow ups. The strength of tools like these is the flexibility and customisation available. It makes it easy to structure information to keep everything accessible.
- **Otter.ai and Teams record and transcribe**: Realtime transcription service that captures conversations and turns them into searchable, shareable notes. These tools reduce the need for manual notetaking so participants can stay fully engaged in discussions.

All-rounder tools

Versatile platforms that integrate scheduling, preparation, documentation and follow up all in one place:

- **Microsoft Loop**: A dynamic workspace designed for real time collaboration. Loop lets you share flexible, portable components like polls (like Doodle, these can be used for nominating meeting times) agendas, action items and status updates. This tool has seamless integration across most Microsoft apps, including Outlook, Teams and OneNote, making it an ideal tool for keeping materials organised and accessible no matter where you are working from.
- **Microsoft Copilot**: An AI-powered assistant integrated into Microsoft 365 apps. Copilot can draft meeting agendas, summarise email threads, generate action items from notes and transcript, and even provide basic data analysis, saving you hours of manual work and helping you stay ahead.
- **Coda**: A flexible document tool that helps you combine text, tables and even interactive elements. You can build all kinds of

documents from agendas to task lists and follow up dashboards all in one interactive document. It reduces app switching and keeps your workflows streamlined and simple.

These tools can save you an enormous amount of time by automating repetitive and time-consuming manual tasks. Knowing how to use these tools effectively allows you to focus more on the high-impact, strategic work that makes you an invaluable member of your organisation.

These tools can be a game changer for managing stress by creating clear, organised workflows and reducing the time you spend on fiddly administrative firefighting. When everything is kept organised and accessible automatically there is less risk of miscommunication or overlooked information.

Automated reminders and real-time updates ensure that you and your executive stay aligned and prepared, minimising the last-minute scrambles and the pressure of tracking all the moving parts.

Collaboration becomes easier and more effective with these tools, as shared workspaces and real-time editing allow for more dynamic and agile changes to be made on the fly.

Whether you're building an agenda in Microsoft Loop, assigning action items in Fellow, or sharing meeting notes in Notion, everyone involved has visibility and input. This transparency fosters accountability and ensures that meetings translate into meaningful actions.

Tech for wellbeing

When you are experiencing burnout, it is sometimes easier to focus on work-based solutions than the mental and emotional recovery we need to do. Thankfully, technology can be a powerful ally for maintaining balance and supporting your mental health.

Special mention: Finch Care.

Finch Care is a fun tool that helps you manage and prevent burnout. Our roles require us to stay ahead of everyone else, which can sometimes leave us with little time to check in with ourselves.

Finch Care helps by providing a gentle, engaging way to prioritise your own mental health. Through its gamified approach, you care for a virtual pet that thrives as you invest in your self-care, turning personal growth into something light-hearted and rewarding.

For Executive Assistants managing burnout, one of the most valuable features of Finch Care is its focus on mindfulness and intentional reflection. You can set daily wellness goals like taking breaks, practicing gratitude or setting boundaries around your work hours. It also encourages journaling and mood tracking, helping you recognise patterns of stress before they escalate into burnout.

By gradually building consistent self-care habits, Finch Care creates space for balance in your day. The app's gentle reminders and positive reinforcement keep you motivated without adding pressure, making it easier to prioritise your wellbeing alongside your responsibilities.

Mental health and mindfulness

- **Headspace**: A popular meditation and mindfulness app that offers guided sessions to reduce stress, improve focus, and help you unwind. Even just a few minutes a day can help you manage anxiety and stay centred during busy workdays.
- **Calm**: Great for relaxation, with meditation, sleep stories, and breathing exercises. It's perfect for decompressing after a long day or taking a quick mental reset between meetings.
- **Insight Timer**: A free meditation app with thousands of guided sessions, music tracks, and talks from wellness experts. It's flexible and offers something for every schedule and mood.
- **RescueTime**: A time-tracking app that helps you understand where your time goes. It gives insight into productivity patterns and helps identify distractions, so you can manage your workload more effectively.

For setting boundaries and protecting focus

- **Forest**: A focus app that encourages you to stay off your phone and concentrate on deep work. As you focus, a virtual tree grows — and if you leave the app early, the tree withers. It's a fun, visual way to manage screen time and stay productive.
- **Freedom**: Blocks distracting websites and apps during work hours. It helps you maintain focus and avoid the temptation of social media or unnecessary browsing.

For physical well-being

- **Streaks**: A habit-tracking app that helps you build and maintain healthy routines — like staying hydrated, taking breaks or stretching during long workdays. Consistency with small habits can make a big difference in managing stress.
- **Stand Up!**: A simple app that reminds you to take movement breaks throughout the day. Perfect for countering long hours at your desk and keeping your energy up.
- **MyFitnessPal**: Tracks meals, water intake, and exercise — helping you stay mindful of your physical health, which directly impacts your energy and resilience at work.

Each of these apps serves a different need, but together they create a well-rounded approach to burnout prevention. By managing your time, protecting your focus, and taking care of your mind and body, you set yourself up for long-term success — and a more balanced, fulfilling work life.

CHAPTER 11
Life audits

A life audit is a transformative exercise that allows you to step back and assess how well each area of your life is aligned with your values, needs and desires.

A comprehensive reflection offers a holistic view of your well-being and allows you to approach life more intentionally. Let's expand on each area of the audit with more detailed focus, addressing key elements that contribute to each body's health.

A life audit can be an incredibly powerful tool when you're experiencing burnout because it helps you step back from the overwhelm and see the bigger picture. Burnout often makes everything feel urgent and exhausting, and it's easy to lose sight of what's working and what isn't.

By examining the four 'bodies' — physical, emotional, mental and spiritual — you can gain insight into where you're thriving and where you need to make adjustments.

By breaking down your life into the four bodies, you can pinpoint the specific areas that need attention and care. This kind of clarity is crucial when you're feeling depleted, as it allows you to focus your energy on the adjustments that will have the greatest impact on your well-being.

One of the biggest benefits of a life audit during burnout is that it helps you distinguish between what you can and can't control.

When you're exhausted, it's easy to feel powerless — like everything is happening to you. But by assessing your physical health, emotional connections, mental growth and sense of purpose, you start to see where you can take small, meaningful steps toward balance.

Maybe it's creating a more supportive workspace, reconnecting with people who uplift you, or setting boundaries around your time and energy. These changes, even when small, build a sense of agency and forward momentum.

A life audit also helps validate your experience. Burnout often brings feelings of inadequacy or self-doubt, but when you take the time to assess your life holistically, you might realise that certain imbalances—not personal failings—are at the root of your exhaustion.

Maybe your physical health has taken a backseat, or your emotional body is drained from a lack of supportive relationships. Recognising these gaps with compassion allows you to address them without self-judgement and focus on recovery with kindness and intention.

Finally, a life audit brings hope. When you're burned out, it's easy to feel stuck—like the only solution is walking away from everything. But by identifying areas of strength and areas for growth, you begin to see that improvement is possible without a complete overhaul.

You don't necessarily need to quit your job or start over; sometimes, small shifts—like creating a morning routine that grounds you, seeking professional development that excites you, or reconnecting with your values—can breathe new life into your current circumstances.

This sense of possibility makes the path forward feel more manageable and reminds you that burnout is a state you can recover from, not a permanent condition.

Let's break down the focus areas.

PHYSICAL

Physical well-being

When considering the physical body, the first and most obvious factor is your physical health. How are you feeling on a day-to-day basis? Are you experiencing fatigue, aches or illnesses that are holding you back from fully engaging in your life and work?

It's essential to take a hard look at your physical state—whether that's through regular health check-ups, tracking energy levels or noting any physical limitations.

Take inventory of how you're treating your body. Are you fuelling it with nourishing foods, staying hydrated and getting enough sleep? Perhaps you're skipping meals or staying up too late, which could be contributing to chronic exhaustion.

Regular physical movement is also crucial for maintaining a healthy body. Reflect on your exercise habits and consider whether they're sufficient for your needs. Small but consistent changes, such as prioritising sleep and making time for exercise, can significantly improve how you feel physically.

Finances

Physical well-being isn't limited to just your body; it also extends to your financial situation.

A significant stressor that often goes unnoticed in life audits is the state of your finances. Are you living pay cheque to pay cheque? Are you carrying a lot of debt or spending beyond your means? These financial pressures can weigh heavily on your physical well-being.

Start by reviewing your expenses, savings and financial goals. Are you living in a way that aligns with your values, or are you overspending on things that don't bring you joy or fulfillment?

Consider setting a budget that reflects both your needs and your aspirations. Small adjustments—like cutting back on unnecessary expenses or investing in your future—can reduce stress and improve your physical sense of security.

Physical environments

The environment around you plays a significant role in how you feel physically.

Take a look at your immediate surroundings—your home, your workspace, and any other places you frequent regularly. Are these spaces conducive to your well-being?

Cluttered, disorganised spaces can create stress and drain energy, whereas clean, organised and intentional environments can uplift you.

Reflect on how your physical environment impacts your mood and productivity. Are you making time to create spaces that reflect your values, help you relax, and foster positive energy? Consider whether your physical spaces support your well-being or if adjustments are needed to create a more harmonious environment.

EMOTIONAL

Fun and recreation

Your emotional well-being is deeply connected to how much joy and fun you experience in life. Often, in the pursuit of work and responsibilities, fun and recreation get pushed to the backburner.

It's essential to evaluate whether you're making time for activities that bring you pleasure and recharge your emotional battery. Reflect on how often you engage in activities that make you smile, laugh and feel carefree.

Whether indulging in a hobby, traveling or spending time with loved ones, nurturing your emotional body involves prioritising moments of fun and enjoyment. A healthy emotional body needs regular breaks from the grind to reset, so be sure to make time for fun without guilt.

Marriage and close relationships

In the emotional body, your relationship with your partner or significant other plays a key role.

Take time to reflect on the quality of your marriage or partnership. Is the connection strong, and are you both communicating openly and honestly? Are you supportive of each other's needs and growth?

Sometimes, in the hustle of everyday life, relationships can feel neglected. A life audit will reveal if you're prioritising your relationship and addressing any unresolved issues that might be creating emotional strain.

If there are gaps in communication or unmet needs, it's time to address them thoughtfully to ensure that your relationship remains a source of emotional support and strength.

Family and friends

Beyond romantic relationships, emotional well-being is supported by your relationships with family and friends.

Take stock of your interactions with loved ones. Are you nurturing connections that provide mutual support and understanding, or are you allowing relationships to fall into patterns of obligation rather than connection?

A lack of meaningful connections can lead to emotional isolation. Consider whether you are investing enough time and energy into your relationships with family and friends.

Reflect on whether there are people in your life who contribute positively to your emotional state or if there are relationships that may be draining you.

Foster stronger connections by reaching out, spending quality time, and setting boundaries with people who may not be supportive.

MENTAL

Mental health

Mental health is foundational to everything in your life.

This area of your audit involves assessing how well you're taking care of your mental and emotional needs. Are you overwhelmed, anxious, or frequently battling negative thoughts? Or are you able to stay grounded, calm and clear-headed, even when faced with challenges?

Pay attention to the signals your mind is sending you. Are you allowing stress to accumulate, or are you actively practicing strategies to manage your mental health, like therapy, mindfulness or stress reduction exercises?

Your mental health is as important as your physical health, and addressing any challenges early on can help you maintain a sense of clarity and balance in all areas of life.

Career

Your career is often the mental focus of much of your time and energy.

In your audit, it's essential to take stock of your current job and career trajectory. Are you feeling fulfilled and motivated in your work? Or do you feel stuck, burned out or disillusioned?

Reflect on how your career aligns with your values, aspirations and long-term goals. If you're feeling stagnant, it might be time to reevaluate whether you need to pursue new opportunities, seek additional training, or have a conversation with your executive about your current workload and goals.

Creating a clear picture of where you want your career to go is essential to your mental well-being. Setting intentions and aligning your work with your passions and strengths can lead to greater satisfaction and productivity.

Personal development

Mental growth doesn't stop once you've reached a certain point in your career.

A life audit encourages you to assess your commitment to personal development and lifelong learning. Are you actively pursuing opportunities for growth, such as professional development, new skills or hobbies that stimulate your intellect?

Personal development is about keeping your mind engaged and continuously striving to improve. Whether it's learning new technologies, expanding your expertise in your field, or simply engaging in activities that challenge your thinking, a life audit helps you gauge whether you're investing in yourself and your growth.

Continuous learning enhances your mental resilience and boosts your confidence in both personal and professional settings.

SPIRITUAL

Spirit and soul

The spiritual body relates to your connection to something larger than yourself. It's about nurturing the part of you that seeks meaning, purpose and fulfillment.

In your life audit, consider whether you feel spiritually connected to your deeper values or if you're going through the motions without reflection. Reflect on your sense of purpose — are you living in alignment with what you believe is meaningful?

If you're struggling with feelings of disconnection or lack of purpose, it's essential to explore ways to re-establish that spiritual connection. Whether through meditation, prayer or self-reflection, nurturing the spirit and soul is about engaging in practices that nourish your deeper sense of self and bring fulfillment.

Community

Spirituality is often enhanced through connection with others. Your community — whether that's your local community, religious group or a broader social circle — provides a sense of belonging and purpose.

Assess how your involvement with your community impacts your spiritual well-being. Do you feel supported and uplifted by those around you, or do you feel disconnected? Strong community bonds can reinforce your sense of belonging and purpose.

If you're feeling isolated, seek out opportunities to engage with like-minded individuals or groups that share your values. Whether that's through volunteering, attending spiritual services, or connecting with friends and family, community plays an important role in spiritual fulfillment.

Purpose or connection to religion

A life audit should also explore your connection to a sense of higher purpose or religion, if that is a part of your life. How connected do you feel to your faith or belief system? Are you actively practicing or reflecting on your spiritual beliefs, or is it something you've let slide?

This connection often brings clarity, peace and direction, helping you navigate challenges with greater resilience.

If spirituality or religion is important to you, take time to reflect on how well you're honouring this part of your life. Whether it's through prayer, reading spiritual texts or participating in community services, actively engaging in your spiritual practice can bring greater meaning and fulfillment to your life.

Bringing it all together

A life audit is about looking at the big picture. By assessing each of the 'bodies' in detail — physical, emotional, mental, and spiritual — you can uncover areas that need attention and adjust your priorities accordingly.

This holistic view of life helps you approach healing and growth from a place of balance, ensuring that all areas of your life are aligned with your needs, values and goals.

The ultimate goal of the audit is to create a life that feels fulfilling, connected and energised, where each of your bodies is well cared for and in harmony with the others.

PHYSICAL
Physical Wellbeing

1. On a scale of 1 to 10, how well do you nourish your body with food that supports your energy, focus and long-term health? What changes could you make to improve this? _____

_____
_____
_____
_____

2. How would you rate your current level of physical activity in supporting your mobility, strength, and overall wellness? What's stopping you from moving more in ways you enjoy? _____

_____
_____
_____
_____

3. How well do you prioritise rest and recovery, including sleep and relaxation? What patterns or behaviours are impacting this? _____

_____
_____
_____
_____

Total score: _____

PHYSICAL
Finances

1. How secure and in control do you feel over your financial situation (income, savings, debt, and future planning) on a scale of 1 to 10? What would move you closer to a 10? _____

_____
_____
_____
_____

2. To what extent does your current income support the lifestyle you want, both now and in the future? What adjustments would make the biggest difference? _____

_____
_____
_____
_____

3. How aligned are your spending habits with your values and long-term goals? Where do you feel pressure around money? _____

_____
_____
_____
_____

Total score: _____

PHYSICAL
Physical Environment

1. On a scale of 1 to 10, how much does your workspace support your productivity and wellbeing? What would make it more functional or enjoyable? _____

_____
_____
_____
_____

2. How well does your home environment reflect comfort, organisation and personal expression? What small changes could enhance it? _____

_____
_____
_____
_____

3. How much does your daily environment (including clutter, lighting and surroundings) impact your stress levels? What's one thing you could improve? _____

_____
_____
_____
_____

Total score: _____

EMOTIONAL
Fun and Recreation

1. How satisfied are you with the amount of time you dedicate to hobbies and activities that bring you joy? What's one thing you'd love to do more of? _____

_____
_____
_____
_____

2. On a scale of 1-10, how often do you allow yourself to truly unwind and have fun? What's stopping you from prioritising play? _____

_____
_____
_____
_____

3. How often do you step away from work and responsibilities to do things purely for your own enjoyment? What's one way you can make this easier? _____

_____
_____
_____
_____

Total Score: _____

EMOTIONAL
Marriage and close relationships

1. How would you rate the level of connection, communication, and support in your closest relationship? What's one way you could strengthen it? _____

2. On a scale of 1-10, how well do you and your partner navigate stress, conflict, and major decisions together? What's one area that could be improved? _____

3. How much does your relationship contribute to your sense of happiness and security? What's something you appreciate about it, and what's one thing you wish were different? _____

Total score: _____

EMOTIONAL

Family and Friends

1. How satisfied are you with the depth and quality of your relationships with family and close friends? Where do you feel a gap? _____

_____
_____
_____
_____
_____

2. On a scale of 1 to 10, how well do you maintain meaningful connections despite the demands of your role? What's one small way you could nurture them more? _____

_____
_____
_____
_____
_____

3. How supported and understood do you feel by the people closest to you? What's one way you could strengthen your social circle? _____

_____
_____
_____
_____
_____

Total score: _____

MENTAL
Mental Health

1. How would you rate your ability to manage stress and prevent overwhelm in your daily life? What's your biggest trigger? _____

_____
_____
_____
_____
_____

2. On a scale of 1 to 10, how balanced do your emotions feel on a regular basis? What coping mechanisms support or hinder your wellbeing? _____

_____
_____
_____
_____
_____

3. How well do you prioritise activities that nourish your mental health (such as therapy, journaling, mindfulness or relaxation)? What's one thing that could help? _____

_____
_____
_____
_____
_____

Total score: _____

MENTAL
Career

1. How fulfilled and challenged do you feel in your current role? What's missing that would make it more rewarding? _____

_____
_____
_____
_____

2. On a scale of 1 to 10, how well does your job align with your values, strengths and long-term career aspirations? Where do you feel friction? _____

_____
_____
_____
_____

3. How supported do you feel in your workplace, both professionally and personally? What's one thing that could improve your work experience? _____

_____
_____
_____
_____

Total score: _____

MENTAL
Personal Development

1. How would you rate your level of growth and learning in the past year? What's one skill or area of knowledge you'd love to deepen? _____

_____
_____
_____
_____
_____

2. On a scale of 1 to 10, how often do you step outside your comfort zone to challenge yourself? What's one fear or limiting belief holding you back? _____

_____
_____
_____
_____
_____

3. How much time do you dedicate to self-reflection and personal growth? What's one mindset shift that could help you thrive? _____

_____
_____
_____
_____
_____

Total score: _____

SPIRITUAL
Spirit and Soul

1. On a scale of 1 to 10, how clearly do you understand who you are beyond your job, relationships, and responsibilities? What are your greatest strengths? _____

_____
_____
_____
_____

2. How aligned do your daily actions feel with your core beliefs and values? Where do you notice disconnects? _____

_____
_____
_____
_____

3. On a scale of 1 to 10, how often do you experience moments of deep peace, purpose, or spiritual connection? What practices help you cultivate this? _____

_____
_____
_____
_____
_____

Total score: _____

SPIRITUAL

Community

1. How would you rate your sense of belonging within a community or network? What's one way you could strengthen that connection? _____

_____
_____
_____
_____

2. On a scale of 1 to 10, how much do you contribute to or engage with the people around you in a meaningful way? Where do you see an opportunity to give back? _____

_____
_____
_____
_____

3. How well does your current social or professional circle reflect the kind of people who inspire and support you? What's one step toward deepening those connections? _____

_____
_____
_____
_____

Total score: _____

SPIRITUAL
Purpose or connection to religion

1. How clear and connected do you feel to a deeper sense of purpose in your life and work? What, if anything, feels missing? _____

_____
_____
_____
_____
_____

2. On a scale of 1 to 10, how aligned do your daily choices feel with what you believe your life's purpose or calling is? What's one adjustment that could bring you closer? _____

_____
_____
_____
_____
_____

3. How fulfilling is your current spiritual or religious practice (if applicable)? What's one way you could deepen this connection or explore it further? _____

_____
_____
_____
_____
_____

Total score: _____

Wheel diagram with categories: Physical Body (Physical Environment, Finances, Physical Wellbeing), Emotional Body (Fun and Recreation, Intimacy, Friends and Family), Spiritual Body (Purpose, Community, Soul), Mental Body (Skills, Mental Health, Career).

What areas currently need extra attention?

_____

_____

_____

What is one thing that you can do today to improve your most challenging category?

_____

_____

CHAPTER 12
Vision boards

Vision boards are powerful tools for creating clarity around your goals and aspirations, especially when you're looking to bring more focus to specific aspects of your life.

They serve as visual representations of your dreams, helping you to focus on what you want to manifest in your life. By using images, words and symbols that resonate with your goals, a vision board can keep you grounded in your intentions and motivate you to make meaningful changes.

When you're feeling overwhelmed or uncertain, a vision board can serve as a visual reminder of your 'why', helping you refocus on your goals.

Creating separate vision boards for each of these aspects outlined below — how you want to feel at work, what an average day looks like, and what a good day looks like — helps you clarify and define your intentions in a deeper, more focused way.

By visualising how you want to feel at work, you align your mindset with the emotions and qualities that will support your overall well-being. This board helps reinforce a positive work atmosphere, which in turn can influence your energy and productivity.

A vision board focusing on your average day provides a roadmap for your routines and structure, ensuring that your workday is organised and manageable. It helps identify potential stressors and solutions to minimise them.

Finally, a vision board dedicated to what a good day looks like serves as a reminder of your professional aspirations — what success, satisfaction and fulfillment in your role should feel like.

By creating separate vision boards for these subheadings, you ensure you are cultivating a work life that reflects both your desires and your values, bringing clarity, motivation and a stronger sense of purpose to your daily experience.

How do I want to feel at work?

When creating a vision board with a focus on how you want to feel at work, the first step is to reflect on the emotions you wish to experience on a daily basis.

For example, do you want to feel empowered, respected, calm and balanced in your role as an Executive Assistant? Are there specific qualities like confidence, clarity and resilience that you wish to embody in your work?

Start by collecting images and words that represent these feelings. It could be pictures of calm, organised spaces, affirmations of empowerment or symbols of leadership.

As you build your vision board, be intentional about creating an emotional landscape that supports your personal and professional well-being. This board will remind you to align your actions, mindset and boundaries with the feelings you want to cultivate in your workplace.

Kathleen Harvey

My workplace feels like …

What does an average day look like?

An average day at work can often feel predictable, even mundane. This activity is intended to be deeply unambitious.

When you are recovering from burnout it can be hard to tell an average day from a bad day. This activity will give you a stronger sense of what normal is. When completing this vision board, it's important to focus on setting a realistic view of your daily routine, rather than aiming for perfection.

Consider how your workday typically unfolds and what aspects of it are within your locus of control. What time do you begin your day, and when does it wrap up? How do you organise your tasks in a way that feels achievable, even if things get a little off track?

Think about including images that represent a balanced and practical workflow, like a manageable to-do list, designated time slots for specific tasks, and moments for breaks throughout the day. Rather than trying to eliminate all stress, aim to visualise yourself moving through the day with a sense of control, knowing how to adjust when things shift.

This vision board will act as a blueprint for creating a realistic, balanced routine that's sustainable and aligns with both your professional responsibilities and personal needs.

If you choose to do one vision board, this should be it. If you only envision a good day, most days can feel like failure and the line between average or normal days, and bad days becomes increasingly blurred.

Kathleen Harvey

A normal day looks like …

What does a good day look like?

When creating a vision board to illustrate what a good day at work looks like, aim for a day where everything aligns with your values and needs. Picture yourself accomplishing tasks effortlessly, managing your time well, and feeling deeply satisfied by your contributions.

A good day might include moments of creativity, positive interactions with your executive or team, and the ability to step away from work at the end of the day feeling fulfilled.

Collect images that evoke feelings of accomplishment, joy and ease. This could be a photo of a team celebrating a project completion, a reminder of your goals being achieved, or an image of a peaceful moment at the end of the day.

By building this vision board, you give yourself a clear image of what a 'successful' day at work looks like, and you can strive to make that a reality on occasion.

In essence, vision boards can help you hone in on how you want to feel, what your daily routine should encompass, and what a successful day looks like for you.

Whether you're aiming for balance, productivity or deeper satisfaction, a vision board serves as a powerful visual tool to manifest your ideal work life.

Kathleen Harvey

A perfect workday looks like …

CHAPTER 13
Boundaries worksheet

This worksheet is designed to help you identify, communicate and maintain boundaries that support both your professional success and personal well-being. By working through each section, you'll gain clarity on where your limits lie, how to express them professionally, and how to reinforce them when challenged.

Use this as a self-reflection tool, a guide for discussions with your executive or team, or even as a resource to revisit when you need a reset.

Remember, boundaries are about what you can control—not about changing others' behavior. You can't stop someone from making last-minute requests, but you can decide how you respond. Use this worksheet as a self-reflection tool, a guide for discussions with your executive or team, or a resource to revisit when you need a reset.

Boundaries aren't about saying 'no' to your job—they're about saying 'yes' to sustainable success.

1. Understanding your boundaries

What are my current pain points? *(Examples: Constant after-hours emails, last-minute requests, unrealistic workloads)*

_____
_____
_____
_____
_____
_____
_____

Which boundaries do I struggle with most?

☐ Work hours ☐ Email and messaging ☐ Unrealistic deadlines ☐ Workload

☐ Personal time ☐ Emotional labour ☐ Respect from colleagues

☐ Other: _____

_____
_____
_____
_____

What physical, emotional, and mental signs tell me my boundaries are being crossed? *(Examples: Exhaustion, frustration, resentment, headaches, loss of motivation)*

_____
_____
_____
_____
_____

2. Defining your boundaries

What is my ideal work-life balance? *(Example: 'I want to leave work at 5 pm without checking emails until the next workday.')*

_____
_____
_____
_____
_____
_____

What boundaries do I need to set to protect my well-being and productivity? *(Example: 'I will not respond to non-urgent emails outside my working hours.')*

_____
_____
_____
_____
_____
_____

What exceptions am I comfortable making, if any? *(Example: 'I will check emails once at 8 pm when my executive is traveling internationally.')*

_____
_____
_____
_____
_____

3. Communicating boundaries effectively

How can I clearly and professionally communicate my boundaries?
(Examples: 'I'm happy to assist, but I need at least 24 hours' notice for scheduling meetings.' or 'I do not check emails after 6 pm. If it's urgent, please call me instead.')

_____
_____
_____
_____

How will I reinforce my boundaries when they are challenged?
(Example: 'I understand this is urgent, but I already have commitments. I can help first thing tomorrow.')

_____
_____
_____
_____

What pushback do I expect, and how will I handle it?
(Example: 'If my executive continues to email after hours, I will address it in my next one-on-one.')

_____
_____
_____
_____

4. Maintaining boundaries in a high-pressure role

What systems or tools can support my boundaries?

☐ Calendar blocking

☐ Auto-replies for after-hours emails

☐ Delegation strategies

☐ Pre-written scripts for saying 'no'

☐ Accountability partner (colleague, mentor, coach)

☐ Other: _____

_____
_____
_____

How will I hold myself accountable for enforcing my boundaries? *(Examples: Weekly self-check-in, journaling, asking a mentor to support me)*

_____
_____
_____
_____
_____

What is my plan if my boundaries continue to be disregarded? *(Examples: Escalating the issue, seeking HR support, re-evaluating my role)*

_____
_____
_____
_____

CHAPTER 14
Documenting conversations

Using the Record of Conversation Template creates a shared, accurate record of important workplace conversations. Whether you're documenting a check-in, a performance discussion, or a sensitive issue, this template helps ensure clarity, accountability and follow-through.

Start by recording the date of the conversation to anchor it in time. This provides a reliable reference if you need to look back later. Note the location too, whether it was in person, online or over the phone. This can affect the perceived tone or context of the discussion.

List all participants, including names and roles. This keeps the record transparent and confirms who was involved in the conversation. Then summarise the subject or purpose. Think of this as setting the scene. What prompted the conversation, and what did everyone come together to discuss? This can be done ahead of the meeting and acts as an indication of whether the conversation was effective or if things got off track.

In the summary of outcomes, focus on capturing the key points and agreements. This section is crucial for reducing misunderstandings. Aim for clear, factual language that reflects what was said and decided, not just how it felt.

Next, outline any actions taken. This might include steps completed during the meeting or immediate follow-ups that were agreed upon. It shows momentum and helps everyone stay aligned.

Finally, note if a review is scheduled. Setting a clear date or timeframe for follow-up keeps things moving and signals that the conversation is part of an ongoing process, not a one-off exchange.

Ultimately, this template is about protecting relationships, supporting good communication, and creating a record that everyone can trust. It helps make sure that what's discussed doesn't get forgotten and that commitments are seen through.

Record of conversation

Date: _____

Location: _____

Participants/ Attendees: _____

_____

_____

Notes taken by: _____

Subject/ Purpose of discussion:

_____

_____

_____

Summary of outcomes:

_____

_____

_____

_____

_____

Actions taken:

_____

_____

_____

Review scheduled: _____

CHAPTER 15
Brain dumps

If you're recovering from burnout, mental clutter can feel overwhelming and paralysing. This brain dump process helps create clarity by getting everything out of your head and onto paper without judgment, pressure, or urgency. From there, you'll gently triage tasks so you can focus your energy where it's most needed.

This version of a brain dump uses the parking lot method for organising thoughts. These are simply suggested zones but for your work and the organisation you work for, you may like to adjust or tailor the categories in step two to better suit your needs.

Step 1: List all tasks on the left

Write down everything that's on your mind; work tasks, personal errands, half-finished ideas, reminders or worries. Don't organise or prioritise yet. Just list it all in the left-hand column of the template. You can do this all at once or as things come up through the day.

When you're burnt out, your brain tries to juggle too much. Getting it out on paper reduces cognitive overload and gives you breathing room, and having one specific place that it goes means you don't need to worry about missing things.

Step 2: Highlight tasks that feel urgent or achievable

Review your list and highlight, or star, the items that feel:

- **Urgent** (with real or perceived deadlines), or
- **Achievable** (even small things you have the capacity to do today)

You don't need to act on everything right now, this is just about identifying what *might* be manageable today.

Burnout can distort your sense of what's important. This step helps reconnect you with realistic priorities and small wins that build momentum.

Step 3: Write the identified tasks onto sticky notes

For each task you've highlighted, write a sticky note or index card. You can add a bit more detail if it helps (e.g. 'Call printer' becomes 'Call printer re: posters for event'). Keep one task per note.

Breaking tasks into visual, moveable pieces keeps things flexible. It also helps you avoid multi-tasking and decision fatigue.

Step 4: Sort the sticky notes into the following categories

Use boxes, sections of your desk, or areas of the page to sort each task into one of the following:

- **Must do** High-priority tasks with direct consequences if left undone
- **Could do** Lower-stakes tasks that are useful but not urgent
- **Want to do** Tasks that light you up or bring you peace/joy
- **Due today** Anything with a same-day deadline
- **Follow up** Tasks where you're waiting on someone or need to check in
- **Scheduling** Tasks that require finding a time slot or booking something
- **Discuss with Executive** Tasks that need a decision, advice or input from your exec
- **Create** Anything involving drafting, designing or building something new.

Categorising tasks lets you see the big picture without getting stuck in panic mode. It also gives you permission to set aside things that don't need immediate action.

You don't have to do everything. You don't even have to finish your 'Must do' pile today. This method is about reconnecting with clarity, giving yourself choices, and moving forward with kindness and intention.

Let this be a tool that supports your healing, not another system to 'get right'.

Kathleen Harvey

Tasks

Must do

Could do

Want to do

Due today	Discuss with Executive

Follow up	

Scheduling	Create

CITATIONS

Online sources

Seppy. (2022, February 10). *Life audit template.* Happier by Seppy. https://www.happierbyseppy.com

Base. (2024, July 29). *How to overcome burnout and reignite your passion as an executive assistant.* Base. https://basehq.com/resources/how-to-overcome-burnout-and-reignite-your-passion-as-an-executive-assistant/

Boldly. (2024, July 29). *Why do executive assistants leave? Three causes of high turnover.* Boldly. https://boldly.com/blog/why-do-executive-assistants-leave/

Office Dynamics. (2024, July 29). *Strategies to overcome burnout as an executive assistant.* Office Dynamics. https://officedynamics.com/strategies-to-overcome-burnout-as-an-executive-assistant/

Executive Leadership Support. (2024, July 29). *Avoiding job burnout as an executive assistant.* Executive Leadership Support. https://teamels.com/avoiding-job-burnout-as-an-executive-assistant/

Reddit. (2024, July 29). *Is this normal or is this burnout? Pace of current role has me seriously considering my career and life decisions.* Reddit. https://www.reddit.com/r/ExecutiveAssistants/comments/17g8opq/is_this_normal_or_is_this_burnout_pace_of_current/

WebMD. (2024, July 29). *Burnout: Symptoms, risk factors, prevention, treatment.* WebMD. https://www.webmd.com/mental-health/burnout-symptoms-signs

Mayo Clinic. (2024, July 29). *Job burnout: How to spot it and take action.* Mayo Clinic. https://www.mayoclinic.org/healthy-lifestyle/adult-health/in-depth/burnout/art-20046642

World Health Organization. (2019, May 28). *Burn-out an 'occupational phenomenon': International classification of diseases.* WHO. https://www.who.int/news/item/28-05-2019-burn-out-an-occupational-phenomenon-international-classification-of-diseases

Mental Health First Aid Australia. (2024, July 29). *Navigating burnout.* MHFA Australia. https://www.mhfa.com.au/navigating-burnout/

Beyond Blue. (2024, December 29). *Burnout, stress and mental health at work*. Beyond Blue. https://www.beyondblue.org.au/mental-health/work/burnout

Allianz Australia. (2024, December 29). *Beyond burnout: A holistic guide to workplace wellbeing and prevention*. Allianz Australia. https://www.allianz.com.au/content/dam/onemarketing/aal/au_site/documents/workers-comp/Burnout-Prevention-Resource_v9-Tagged.pdf

MindHealth PHN. (2025, February 12). Help for people coping with stress management. MindHealth PHN. https://mindhealth.org.au/mental-health-issues/stress-management/

Black Dog Institute. (2025, February 12). *Experiencing burnout? Here's what to do about it*. Black Dog Institute. https://www.blackdoginstitute.org.au/news/experiencing-burnout-heres-what-to-do-about-it/

ReachOut Australia. (2025, February 12). *What is burnout? Emotional exhaustion & burnout symptoms*. ReachOut Australia. https://au.reachout.com/challenges-and-coping/stress/what-is-burnout

The Burnout Project. (2025, March 22). *Individual support*. The Burnout Project. https://theburnoutproject.com.au/support/

Australian Psychological Society. (2025, March 22). *Stress in the workplace*. APS. https://psychology.org.au/for-the-public/psychology-topics/stress-in-the-workplace

Australian Psychological Society. (2025, February 22). *Preventing workplace burnout: Why resilience is not enough*. APS. https://psychology.org.au/for-members/publications/inpsych/2018/june-issue-3/preventing-workplace-burnout-why-resilience-is-no

Coolout. (2025, March 27). *How burnout stops: A practical guide to stress management, burnout prevention and burnout recovery*. Coolout. https://www.coolout.co/how-burnout-stops-book

The Anti-Burnout Club. (2025, March 27). Home. The Anti-Burnout Club. https://theantiburnoutclub.com/

Books

Schaufeli, W. B., & Leiter, M. P. (Eds.). (2013). *Burnout for experts: Prevention in the context of living and working*. Springer.

Nagoski, E., & Nagoski, A. (2019). *Burnout: The Secret to Unlocking the Stress Cycle.* Ballantine Books.

Petersen, A. H. (2020). *Can't Even: How Millennials Became the Burnout Generation.* Houghton Mifflin Harcourt.

Hanks, J. de A. (2011). *The Burnout Cure: An Emotional Survival Guide for Overwhelmed Women.* New Harbinger Publications.

Carter, S. B. (2011). *High Octane Women: How Superachievers Can Avoid Burnout.* Prometheus Books.

Haig, M. (2019). *Notes on a Nervous Planet.* Canongate Books.

SafeWork Australia. (2016). *Dealing with Workplace Bullying: A Worker's Guide.* SafeWork Australia.

Burrows, J. (2020). *Leader Assistant Four Pillars of a Confident, Game-Changing Assistant.* Assistants Lead.

Podcasts

Burningham, C., & McBride, J. (Hosts). (n.d.). *The Future Focused Admin* [Audio podcast]. The Future Focused Admin.
https://open.spotify.com/show/55y16Dg7F5drPs5gEhgJux

Kohler, U. (Host). (n.d.). *After 5 with Capital EA* [Audio podcast]. Capital EA.
https://open.spotify.com/show/622KFUslwp0Ciq7j2RqnnI

Vann, J. (Host). (n.d.). *REACH – A Podcast for Executive Assistants* [Audio podcast]. Maven Recruiting Group.
https://open.spotify.com/show/3F5jYEO99617g552b3kAE9

ABOUT THE AUTHOR

Kathleen Harvey is an experienced Executive Assistant, writer, and advocate for workplace well-being. With over 10 years of experience supporting executives across Australian government agencies and non-profits, Kathleen understands the unique challenges EAs face — especially when it comes to burnout.

Drawing from personal experience and professional expertise, she writes practical, compassionate resources that empower assistants to reclaim balance and thrive in their roles.

Outside of work, Kathleen enjoys creative pursuits like sewing, knitting and reading, as well as finding ways to build meaningful connections in her community. She is passionate about helping others feel supported, both professionally and personally, and believes in fostering workplaces where wellbeing is a priority.

Connect with Kathleen on LinkedIn and Instagram to join the conversation on workplace well-being and Executive Assistant success.

NEXT STEP

Organise your
Free Discovery Session
simply visit
www.theEAhandbook.com
to book your free introductory session online.

OFFERINGS

Book | eBook | AudioBook

Keynote Speaking
Events | Conferences | Summits | Webinars | Podcasts

Residential Retreats | Workshops | Seminars

Wellbeing Coaching | Professional Coaching

All offerings are available
LIVE and ONLINE GLOBALLY

Print on demand

All titles by Kathleen Harvey are available at special quantity discounts for bulk purchases to be included for marketing, promotions, fundraisers and/or education purposes.

You could also use them as a giveaway or as a gift with purchase for your valued clients or on the shelf in your library.

Contact **kathleen@theEAhandbook.com** to discuss how we can accommodate your needs.

www.ingramcontent.com/pod-product-compliance
Lightning Source LLC
Chambersburg PA
CBHW070543090426
42735CB00013B/3057